A GIRL FROM
THE HILL

A GIRL FROM THE HILL

MY MOTHER'S JOURNEY FROM ITALIAN GIRL TO AMERICAN WOMAN

PATRICIA L. MITCHELL

BALBOA.
PRESS
A DIVISION OF HAY HOUSE

Balboa Press books may be ordered through booksellers or by contacting:

Balboa Press
A Division of Hay House
1663 Liberty Drive
Bloomington, IN 47403
www.balboapress.com
1-(877) 407-4847

Because of the dynamic nature of the Internet, any web addresses or links contained in this book may have changed since publication and may no longer be valid. The views expressed in this work are solely those of the author and do not necessarily reflect the views of the publisher, and the publisher hereby disclaims any responsibility for them.

The author of this book does not dispense medical advice or prescribe the use of any technique as a form of treatment for physical, emotional, or medical problems without the advice of a physician, either directly or indirectly. The intent of the author is only to offer information of a general nature to help you in your quest for emotional and spiritual well-being. In the event you use any of the information in this book for yourself, which is your constitutional right, the author and the publisher assume no responsibility for your actions.

Any people depicted in stock imagery provided by Thinkstock are models, and such images are being used for illustrative purposes only. Certain stock imagery © Thinkstock.

Printed in the United States of America

ISBN: 978-1-4525-6944-4 (sc)
ISBN: 978-1-4525-6946-8 (hc)
ISBN: 978-1-4525-6945-1 (e)

Library of Congress Control Number: 2013903662

Balboa Press rev. date: 4/22/2013

This book was written for Dahlia and Alphonse, with love and appreciation.

And for Zingarella Lee Mitchell (10/27/1995 – 9/20/2012). I will always miss waking up with your head on my shoulder and your purring in my ear.

ACKNOWLEDGEMENTS

A Girl from the Hill would never have happened without help and support from so many kind, generous people. My eternal gratitude goes out to so many. My friend Lisa Barnstein and my mother-in-law Judy Mitchell worked both diligently and kindly to edit the manuscript. Genealogist and friend Barbara Carroll helped me figure out where the Fiores came from. Book Coach Lisa Tenor inspired and supported me throughout the writing and publishing process. My sisters, Maree O'Brien and Donna Carnevale, helped me gain clarity and graciously supported me. Actually I am blessed all around when it comes to family and friends– I could not ask for a more amazing and supporting group. And then there's my husband Jeremy. He quietly stands by my side and allows me to be who I am meant to be. My daughter Julia knows more at 12 about how to be a good daughter than I probably ever will. And Balboa Press has allowed me to live my dream of becoming a published author. With a grateful heart I thank you all.

TABLE OF CONTENTS

Al and Dale on their honeymoon in New York in 1946.
Ironically, my mother never learned to drive a real car.

PREFACE

I've traveled intense but interesting roads these past two years, trying to understand my mother's life, and our connection as mother and daughter. My family enjoys our privacy, our low, ordinary profiles as working class, mostly blue-collar New Englanders. However, somehow sharing my findings with the world, so to speak, brings a glow of pride to my very being. And I want to see my mother's light shine too, because though ordinary, we are still special, unique and connected with the rest of the world.

I started this journey by helping her write down some of her memories. And then we began to talk, to share and to connect. What I've ended up with is a chronicle of her life through a series of essays that I hope speak to her essence as a daughter, a wife, a mother, and the woman she has become over the past 88 years.

I must stress that these stories are based on my mother's recollections, adapted by me to form the essays included in this book. They are based on her memories, memories not intended to malign, insult, or otherwise be used in a negative context. Neither are they intended for historical research. The exception here is the genealogical information gathered about my family's emigration to the United States, Ellis Island and Rhode Island specifically. All genealogical information has been thoroughly researched and validated using appropriate birth and death certificates, census information, ship manifests and other certified data.

My mother has lived a full life, and in no way have I captured it all here. This book includes some of the highlights, as well as some of the low points, as I struggled to try and figure her out. She's not as easy as she appears. No one really is. And I have tried to find our connection, beyond just the umbilical cord and blood that binds us. There have been days, years when I have felt so removed and distant from her, and other times, like when I was a small child, and now, where I feel like we are different versions of the same person.

A big part of being my mother includes being an Italian American. She was born to Italian parents who came to Ellis Island in the late 19th and early 20th Centuries, settling in Rhode Island during a time when it was brimming with Italian immigrants. The Italian culture, both classical and pedestrian, remains strong and nearly inescapable in this little state to this day. In a wonderful way, of course, as if finding you are surrounded by loyal and trustworthy friends.

The man my mother married, my father, is also Italian American, born to Italian American parents. His grandparents arrived here in the 19th century, making my father a second generation American. But despite the differences in looks and demeanor, you could probably pave a path between their villages in Italy.

Piecing together my mother's genealogy, from San Giovanni Incarico, Italy to first Burrillville, then Providence, Rhode Island could probably result in a different book all together. But, so that you can keep the family straight, it's important to note that my mother had four brothers, Joseph, Constantino, Rinaldo and Roland, and three sisters, Philomena, Assunta, and Alicia.

In order to better understand my Italian American family's roots, and the stories that follow, I've provided a basic family tree depicting most of the main characters in my mother's life. My hope is you are provided with some guidance as you read on.

The Family Tree

5 Generations

Julia Marie Mitchell (b.2000)

Jeremy Thomas Mitchell (b.1966)

Patricia Lynn Mitchell (b.1964)

Donna Jean Carnevale (b.1957)

Jane Ann Coyne (b.1954)

Alphonse Robert Testa Jr. (b.1951)

Maree Arlene O'Brien (b.1947)

Dorothy Testa

Elaine O'Neill

Ann Ionta

Alphonse Robert Testa (b.1921)

Dahlia Lydia Fiore (b.1924)

Philomena Tanzi

Assunta Fiore

Joseph Fiore

Alicia Fiore

Constantino Fiore

Rinaldo Fiore

Roland Fiore

Anthony Testa (1893-1996)

Giovannina DeLuca (1896-1990)

Givoanni Fiore (1874-1958)

Maria Giovanna Mollo (1883-1941)

Alfonso Testa

Maria Testa

Frank DeLuca

Alexandria DeLuca

Guiseppe Fiore

Filomena Martini

Maria Giovanna Renzi

Constantino Richard Mollo

INTRODUCTION: FROM DELICATE FLOWER TO THE OLD CROW

S itting with my mother for the first time to listen formally to her stories and recollections, I held some obvious and unimaginative pre-conceptions. Whether they came from reminiscing whimsically about the good old days, or comparing notes with her brothers and sisters when they all were alive, her stories are not totally unfamiliar. I didn't expect to be shocked or impressed. This will be easy. How deep could she be, really? I was so wrong.

Her life in the early to mid 20[th]century differs from mine now in the 21[st.] But one thing remains constant. Becoming a woman in any age challenges us to either stand up or sit down, to be heard or be stifled. My mother did both, by choice sometimes, but other times because "That's the way it was." I am so fortunate to become a wife and mother in this age versus hers. The path to discover one's identity is rarely an easy one. I am grateful to have her lessons to guide me—even now as I sit at the top of the fence, or the hill, unwilling as any woman to climb over to the other side.

My mother's words are simple. At times I have tried to improve them with more 'colorful' language, more complex descriptions. But I stopped myself more often than not; because reading her words over and over, trying to improve them, I found it difficult to better describe the transformation of this skinny little olive-skinned girl with the big dark eyes and the long chestnut hair—a little girl who adored her family and found solace and comfort in a sprawling Victorian home. A home decorated with carefully selected treasures that served as her source of stability, refuge, and belonging. Over time her universe changed. She lost many of the people and things she adored, only to find herself thrown into a world where she was no longer the youngest, the delicate flower Dahlia. As she morphed from Dahlia to Zat, to Dale, Mommy and Grammy, she came dangerously close to losing herself.

That's when the delicate flower finally stood up and strengthened to become the tough old Crow I love. And that amazes me more each day.

Dahlia still holds those memories of warm mahoganies and lace curtains, and the crevices where a little girl could hide, reading her books and making believe. I'm grateful she has shared them with me, and can't help but grin watching her bask in that sweet glow of happiness. I have my memories too, of a mother I could always cuddle with, a lap that never refused to gently rock me out of whatever drama I conjured. And as my daughter snuggles with me after a long day at school or an intense game of basketball, I hope I can provide her as much comfort as my mother did me, along with the ability to let my little girl go and find her own definition of womanhood.

Giovanni Fiore, aka, "Pop"

A GIRL FROM THE HILL— WHERE IT ALL BEGAN

D ahlia Lydia Fiore was born in Burrillville, Rhode Island on the Fourth of July in 1924, the eighth of eight children—four boys, four girls. Her father Giovanni came to Providence, Rhode Island, from San Giovanni Incarico, a small Italian village that is part of the province of Frosinone, and about an hour north of Naples. After settling in Providence, getting work farming, he sent for his fiancée, Maria Giovanna Mollo. They were married August 3, 1903 at Holy Ghost Church in the Federal Hill section of Providence.

Most of the Italians immigrating to Rhode Island at the turn of the 20th century ended up in or around Federal Hill. You can still find traces of Rhode Island's Little Italy, like Scialo's Bakery, and the Gateway Arch with its *La Pigna* hovering over traffic on Atwells Avenue. While most people refer La Pigna as the "Big Pineapple," on close inspection you'll find that it's actually an ornate pine cone, an Italian symbol for welcome and abundance. Venda Ravioli is still there, under new ownership, but still with the same *cibo delizioso* (delicious food). DePasquale Square and its stone fountain cascading water transports you to a piazza in Rome or Genoa. Holy Ghost Church is still there too, on the corner of Knight Street and Atwells Avenue.

The new Federal Hill also offers Nuevo Italian restaurants, along with Asian grocery stores, tattoo parlors, Indian cuisine and multi-cultural retail. You can still get the best sausage, peppers and onions on a torpedo roll, fried calamari, or creamy cannoli at the Hill's annual Columbus Day festival; only now you can add in Indian Samosas, shrimp fried rice, and sweet and sour chicken to the menu.

In 1924, when the skinny little olive-skinned girl with the big dark eyes and the dark chestnut hair, the eighth of eight came along, Giovanni Fiore already joint-owned a farm in Wakefield RI, close to Narragansett Bay, which feeds out into the Atlantic Ocean. After that came another farm in Harrisville, in the northern corner of the state near Worcester, Massachusetts. Nine months after Dahlia was born, Giovanni decided he wanted his own place, his own house without countless cousins from Italy landing on his doorstep to start a new life on his dime. He couldn't say no to his family, and he regularly provided his people a place to stay, food to eat, and, to his later downfall, he co-signed their loans.

In an attempt to make a fresh start for his own family, Giovanni sold his share of the Harrisville farm to his brother-in-law, Sam Toti, and moved his wife, eight kids, and his brother-in-law Roger to a large Victorian in Providence, at 63 Marshall Street, off Broadway on Federal Hill. Unfortunately, his move to the city did not bring an end to his innate and well-meaning generosity. The red flag of foreclosure would one day stand in his lawn as a result.

Giovanni's lack of technical skills and formal education limited his employment opportunities. He took whatever job he could get in the city. From farming he went to night watchman—first in a jewelry shop, later in a hat factory. Little Dahlia looked forward to waking up each morning to find the new hats her father brought home from his late shift, and she took great joy in modeling navy straw cloches, black mesh slouches with velvet trim, and olive wool turbans for the rest of the family.

While her father worked nights, little Dahlia slept with her mother in her parents' bed. When Dahlia turned five, her oldest sister Philomena married and moved with her new husband Emilio to Boston, where he held a job in a steel mill. Dahlia took Philomena's place in the girls' bedroom, between her other older sisters, Assunta and Alicia. Not a pleasant transition for the skinny little girl who was used to snuggling close to her mother at night to now be stuck between the two teenagers, who instead of providing comfort, provided little Dahlia with a foot or knee jabbed into the small of her back.

She missed those nights with her mother. Dahlia longed for the closeness of her mother always. Unlike me, who adored her mother as a young girl, but then grew distant during adolescence; returning back only once I understood her importance in my life. Dahlia lost Maria too early, and never had the opportunity to grow apart from her. But I think that even if she had that chance, she wouldn't have taken it.

The late 80's, and one of the last pictures of the surviving Fiore Kids.
L to R—Dahlia, Sue, Roland, a family friend, Alice and Reynolds.
Joe, Phil and Danny had passed away by this time.

Among the Fiore kids, Joe (the Bull) and
Sue were the chief disciplinarians.

EVERYBODY HAS A NAME—
OR TWO

For Italians *"Tutti hanno un nome,"* or "Everyone has a name." Surfing around some Italian web sites and blogs one day, I noticed that phrase. Suddenly everything made sense. Italians love to adorn others with *nomignoli,* or nicknames. Usually it's some character trait or physical uniqueness that inspires the nickname. As if the names so carefully chosen by one's parents cannot sufficiently define one's true essence, the nickname provides necessary and adequate compensation.

While Mafia characters used *nomignoli* like The Weasel, The Fish, Scarface, Baby Shacks, my mother's family came up with their own versions. Discussing the nicknames of her siblings and other family friends is where Dahlia and I began sharing her memories for *"A Girl from the Hill."*

Her siblings' nicknames are both amusing and accurate, usually consisting of an Americanization of their given name, plus a bona fide *nomignoli*.

As the oldest boy and the one who took great effort and pride in keeping his siblings in line, her brother Joseph became known not only as Joe, but *The Bull*. That name stuck with him his entire life. Joe was tough and took the lead in disciplining the younger Fiore kids. My memories are that of a sweet, gentle man with a large wrinkly face, a kind but mischievous grin, and huge hands and ears—almost like a gigantic George Burns. My mother adored all of her brothers, but I tend to believe *The Bull* was her favorite.

My aunt Assunta became Sue; my uncle Constantino became . . . Danny. Not sure where that came from, but he possessed a *nomignoli* as well, *The Rabbit*. He was probably the most timid of all the Fiore boys and, according to my mother, constantly pegged as the scape goat for sibling antics.

The third Fiore son, Rinaldo, became Reynolds, or *The Fox*. Still is, as he's the sixth of eight and my mother's only living sibling. She remembers *The Fox* always trying to make a deal, using his brothers as the fall guys. Unlike the Rabbit, the Fiore Fox always managed to end up on top.

My mother's fourth brother, my godfather Roland, became Rolly, also known to family and friends as *The Turk*. This revelation immediately brought the famous scene at Louie's Restaurant in *The Godfather* to my mind, when Michael Corleone shoots the animal-like Sollozzo—aka The Turk—and the corrupt Police Captain McCluskey, and walks out, clumsily shaking the weapon from his sweaty hand while glaring straight ahead in a near trance. Perhaps Italians feared or didn't like something about Turkish people? Did they consider them violent or uncivilized? I know Rolly couldn't have been a savage like Sollozzo. Rolly became *The Turk* because he was the strongest—a boxer, wrestler, and football player during his years at Providence's Central High School.

My mother's other sisters, Philomena and Alicia got Americanized to Phil and Alice, but were too sweet and kind to have nicknames, certainly not based on farm animals or supposed barbarian cultures. And Sue, well, everyone loved Sue, but no one dared come up with a *nomignolo* for her for fear she'd find out and "Knock their blocks off." She was the female counterpart to *The Bull*, though I would never, ever think of calling my Auntie Sue *The Cow*. She took no crap and was probably the most strikingly beautiful of all the sisters, with dark wavy hair and brown eyes like her mother. She had a lung removed when she was 26 and her perseverance in the battle to breathe only added to her tenacity.

Now my mother, Dahlia, assumed many names, and she still does.

Dahlia Lydia Fiore is a beautiful, graceful name. As a flower, each Dahlia bloom explodes with giant bursts of color, created by countless tiny, delicate petals. Dahlias look strong but are especially vulnerable to the elements, especially cold. Fiore means 'flowers' in Italian, Lydia means 'noble" in Greek. Her name evokes visions of nobility as it rolls off my tongue. Just the right measures of mystique, sensuality and sophistication—like a silent movie star or a European super model.

Apparently her contemporaries conjured an alternate vision. When Dahlia started school, people had difficulty pronouncing her name. Instead of making a concerted effort, students and teachers alike made up their own versions of Dahlia—Delia or Della or Delilah or countless other bastardizations my mother doesn't even remember anymore. To add to the confusion, Italian birth certificates apparently place the middle name in front of the first name, at least according to my grandparents. That, along with their 'broken' English, resulted in my mother's birth certificate declaring her Lydia Delia Fiore. Many levels of bureaucratic confusion resulted; first in school, and later when she attempted to exercise her rights to such documents as her marriage license in 1946, her passport in 1974, and later still to her Social Security checks in 1989.

To avoid the confusion at school my mother decided to go by the simpler Dale; easier to pronounce but a lot less elegant. A good solid name Dale is. Boy or girl can use it. Dahlia and Dale both mean *valley*—Dahlia in Swedish and Dale in English. My mother was not aware of this until many years later, long after she decided to androgenize herself. Meanwhile, at home, her mother called her Zahlia, partly as a pet name, partly because she had a hard time pronouncing Dahlia. Her cousins often called her Zallah. She answered to all variations without objection.

As names went, Dahlia juggled more than her share. She created Dale to cut down on the volume and variety of mispronunciations, but her brothers remained a creative bunch. At some point the Fiore boys decided she needed yet one more—a name to stick and not get challenged with an American alternative. Dahlia the Swedish princess, Dale the lumberjack, morphed into—Zat.

I don't know what Zat is supposed to mean. My dad still calls her Zat. My mother doesn't mind it, and never seemed to. She knew that having a nickname in the eyes of her brothers, and her husband, meant that she was loved, no matter how atrocious it sounded. When I asked my mother what Zat meant, she said she wasn't sure. Perhaps it had something to do with water rats, perhaps it's a combo of Zahlia and Zallah and God knows what else. With that many names, I wouldn't have known which way to turn, but my mother answered to it all, more often than not in a kind, patient manner. Unless she didn't feel like it. But we'll get to that.

Assimilation by name took on importance for the Fiores and lots of other Italian-American families of the time. While preparing this book, I laughed to see census reports from the early 20th century listing John and Mary Fiore and their children living in Burriville, Rhode Island. John and Mary, how generic can you get?

When Dahlia Lydia Fiore married Alfonzo Roberto (aka Alphonse Robert) Testa, they made a conscious effort to keep their offspring names all American—though my brother did get stuck with carrying on the tradition of Alphonse—that one screams for a beating in any language.

In our family, *nomigloni* assignment worked on multiple levels. First and foremost was the day-to-day names assigned that followed one simple rule. You see, my parents added an 'e' sound to all of our names, probably to add just the slightest level of pizazz—and nausea, to some very plain names. Marie (who changed her own name to Maree by the way) was lucky because she already had one, but my brother became Alley, Jane became Janey, Donna became Donney, and I became Patty. In second grade I took out the 'e,' and became Pat, another androgynous favorite. Our parents referred to us en masse as "The Indians," most likely due to our raucous manner not unlike those that fought the cavalry. Oh and my Dad had one for me—Mophead—due to the headful of wild banana curls that I inherited from the Fiores. My Dad isn't one to overtly build one's self-esteem, you see, so Mophead was as good as it got. But he did always use it affectionately and with good humor. My other sisters had nicknames but they would probably sue me if I shared them here. Let's just say they had a few special *nomignoli* that both my parents and my brother (carrying on the family tradition) crafted through the years.

My mother certainly wore her share of names, like most mothers do, well perhaps a few more than most mothers. Her little ones called her Mommy during their sweetest times, then in time Ma, and sometimes even the formal Mother depending on the age and mood of any one of her five children. Most of the family still laughs whenever we talk about one of my father's aunts who used to almost purr my mother's name, or something like it. "Gale…Gale…are you making the cookies this year?" She craved my mother's famous platters of Christmas twists, snowballs, cherry-winks and prune cookies as if they were catnip treats meant for her overstuffed Cheshire cat frame. If only she could get the small detail of her name right.

All but one of my mother's 11 grandchildren calls her Grammy, which started with my two oldest nieces back in the late sixties. My daughter is the exception, calling her Mimi. She wanted another word for Mommy for this tiny woman who held her on her knee, repeating her favorite stories over and over on demand and whispering rhymes in Italian to lull her to sleep.

The crowning designation, though, the best by far, is the one my nephew Philip came up with, and it's pretty much the handle we all use now—*Crow.* As a tween he referred to her as *The Old Crow*, partly as a tease and partly as the truth. Despite my mother's gentility and kindness, through the years, her filtering system has sort of … eroded. I don't know if it's time, age, senility, entitlement, or just wanting to break the stereotype, but she comes up with some whoppers that can just knock you off your seat. Many a time I have just longed to plug my ears, close my eyes, and wish myself away. Whether she thinks your shirt is too tight and says "Mercy," making you want to cringe into a corner, or if she spits her gum out on the sidewalk when the ladylike thing would be to place it gingerly in a tissue and then in a convenient trash receptacle. That is *The Crow.* Very few holds are barred with her now—say what's on your mind or don't waste her time. Not a bad thing, but not what you'd expect from this little Grammy.

My nephew Philip (we call him Philly of course) never called his grandmother Crow with malice. This name comes complete with a boatload of affection and endearment.

I'm thinking that Crow is exactly what we should now expect from Zat. Her brothers had her pegged. Zat was quite the imp, indulged and spoiled—who loved to laugh and have fun at anyone and everyone's expense. She loved to make others laugh too. Entertaining her brothers and sisters and her parents was a critical part of her life, whether hiding in the pantry and bleating like a goat while there was company in the house, or tap dancing on the kitchen floor. It all became part of her shtick. Her whole family loved to joke—their best coping mechanism to soften some of the harder blows of life. With little Zat right in the middle of it all, trying to make everyone laugh, make everything good. Make her mother smile.

Of all her names, *The Crow* remains the one my mother wears most proudly, as a badge of honor. Crow, or Crowbie Wan Kenobi as I call her, is a survivor. She went from having an indulgent and coddled childhood, to becoming a teenager and watching the mother she adored lie dying and helpless. She married at a time when women didn't have much say over anything, to a man who was perfectly happy with that arrangement for many, many years. She kept us all going and never got much credit for it. But she was always there. When we got home at the end of the day, making us meals, cleaning our rooms, pushing us forward when I'm sure there were times when she just wanted to stop and unravel. She put everything she had into her family, as she longed for a family like hers on Marshall Street. She tried as hard as she could to be like the mother she adored: charitable, kind, and loved by everyone who knew her. And we tried as hard as we could to make her laugh whenever we weren't busy making her miserable.

It's true that Dahlia is almost never called Dahlia anymore. Sometimes by my father jokingly, sometimes by strangers who don't know about Dale, Zat, or Crow. But she is Dahlia Lydia Fiore Testa now, and maybe she could have been an Italian Swedish princess in another time. All the roles she's played for us have left an indelible mark on us, the people she served, whether we express our appreciation or not. And I think it's even more important to understand what Dahlia felt about her roles, these names bestowed upon her for better and worse. I am happy to say I continue to find little Dahlia within her, despite the years, the fading, the wrinkling and the thinning on the outside. I know she's still there, protected by The Crow.

To read more about Italian nicknames, and the Italian language in general, check out Diane Hale's site "Becoming Italian Word by Word at http://becomingitalianwordbyword.typepad.com/becomingitalian/

L to R—Dahlia, Alice, Reynolds (The Fox) and Sue in front of Phil's house on Rankin Ave in Providence

CHRISTMAS COOKIES—ITALIAN STYLE

My parents couldn't afford to buy everyone Christmas presents each year, but they could invest in flour, eggs, sugar and my mother's elbow grease in order to provide loved ones and my father's closest real estate colleagues each a platter of Christmas cookies. Arranged on tin or plastic platters topped with paper doilies, then wrapped festively with Saran Wrap and curly ribbon, the cookies were my mother's labor of love and good will.

A note about my mother's recipes: My mother's recipes consist of ingredient lists with approximate measurements, baking temperatures, and processing instructions. I've deciphered them as clearly as I can. The full essence of each recipe resides within my mother's head, and in many cases is under lockdown. Despite my thorough interrogations, I cannot fully guarantee complete capture. I've confirmed the recipes included here with my sister Donna, who bakes and sells these treats regularly; so I am confident that the important details are all here. However, I do recommend that you already have some general baking experience before embarking. The fact that my mother still bakes at 88 years old astounds me to the point that the recipes are almost secondary.

Twists

Twists are my mother's specialty and a family favorite. As a girl I enjoyed playing with the little cutting wheel my mother used to cut the dough into ridged strips. (You can use a regular knife if you don't have a tool like this.) Twists are flakey and layered like croissants, but smaller and slightly heavier in texture.

<u>Recipe:</u>

2 cups of butter or margarine
3 eggs
1 package of yeast
1 cup sour cream—or add 1 tsp. of white vinegar to 1 cup of milk to make sour
    milk.
½ tsp. salt
6 cups flour
1 cup granulated sugar; cinnamon can be added to the sugar for variety.
Confectionary (powdered) sugar for sprinkling, once cookies are baked and
    cooled.

- Preheat oven to 375 degrees.
- Mix butter, flour and salt together until grainy.
- Make a well with these ingredients, and then add sour cream/milk and yeast.
- Add in eggs and mix it all into elastic dough.
- Roll dough into a ball and refrigerate for 3 hours. My mother always wraps the ball in wax paper.
- After 3 hours, remove dough from refrigerator and roll it into a rectangle. Don't flour the dough when rolling unless it's simply impossible to work with, and then use only a bit.
- Fold the dough rectangle over three times to make a longer rectangle. Before each fold over, sprinkle granulated sugar on top of the dough, including the very top.
- Flatten the dough with a rolling pin to ½ inch thickness.
- Cut the dough into strips, about ¾ inches wide. Use a knife or small cutting wheel that will crimp the edges.
- Twist two strips of dough together and tie them into a bow-like pretzel shape. For a lighter cookie, twist only one strip at a time into a bow.
- Bake at 375 degrees on an ungreased cookie sheet for 10-12 minutes.
- Loosen cookies from sheet once they come out of the oven, as the sugar can make them stick. You can then cool them on the sheet or move them to a cooling rack.
- Sprinkle with confectionary sugar when cool.

Cherry Winks

Cherry Winks are all-American, but are always included in Italian cookie trays. I'm pretty sure my mother found the recipe on the side of a Corn Flakes box back in the 1950's. The cookies are rolled in crushed cornflakes and adorned with a slice of Maraschino cherry. My memories include cramming my chubby little fingers into jars of red sugary cherries, trying to pilfer as many as possible.

Recipe

2 ¼ cups flour
1 tsp. baking powder
½ tsp. baking soda
¾ cup Crisco or margarine
1 cup sugar
2 eggs
2 tsp. milk
1 tsp. vanilla
2 cups crushed cornflakes
⅓ cup Maraschino cherries, cut in half or quarters
Optional: 1 cup chopped walnuts

- Preheat oven to 350 degrees.
- Mix first three dry ingredients together in order as listed above.
- Add remaining ingredients, except cornflakes and cherries until a dough forms.
- Roll tablespoons full of dough into balls, and then into crushed cornflakes.
- Place on greased cookie sheet.
- Top each cookie with a slice of cherry, pressing down gently in the middle to flatten.
- Bake at 350 degrees on a greased cookie sheet for 10-12 minutes.
- Let cookies set on sheet for a few minutes before moving them to a cooking rack to cool completely.

Italian Molasses Cookies

Italian Molasses cookies resemble gingerbread biscotti, and are probably my mother's most challenging cookie recipe; not because of the ingredients, but because there is no set baking time to document. These cookies taste best when baked to a firm tenderness. The best method to test for doneness is to stick a toothpick through the center of the dough after about 20 minutes or so, and then continually until the toothpick comes out clean. Once it comes out clean, they're done. Italian Molasses cookies are wonderful for dunking into a mug of hot coffee on a cold winter morning.

Recipe:

2 lbs. flour
4 eggs
1 pint of light or dark molasses
¾ cup of sugar
2 tbsp. of vegetable oil
½ tsp. baking powder
½ tsp. baking soda
½ tsp. black pepper
Pinch of salt
Zest of one orange
Yolk of 1 egg

- Preheat oven to 375 degrees.
- Make a well with dry ingredients.
- Add the 4 eggs, molasses, sugar, and oil to center and mix.
- Add pepper and orange rind, and more flour as needed to make soft dough.
- Roll dough into long logs (about 12 inches long) and brush the tops with beaten egg yolk.
- Bake at 375 degrees on greased cookie trays, until toothpick comes out clean from center of each log.

Struffoli (Struveli)

This is my mother's Wandi dough recipe, as she swears it's the same dough for both Wandi and Struffoli. I confirmed with trusted online recipes and relatives, not that I don't trust her, but, you never know with a Crow. Struffoli is by far my favorite Christmas sweet, and in my humble opinion, a true Italian delicacy.

Struffoli is neither cake nor cookie, but an awesome collection of fried dough balls molded together with honey that taste like candy. My Grandma Jenny Testa used to make these and so did my Auntie Dot. I remember how I looked forward to getting a chunk, and chewing into the gooey honey, smacking my lips like Winnie the Pooh as I ate. My mother said both my grandmothers molded their Struffoli into wreath shapes and brought them to friends and family as gifts. Auntie Dot continued her mother's tradition for many years, and would often make one just for me once Grandma Jenny passed away.

<u>Recipe</u>

1 dozen eggs
½ cup of granulated sugar
Zests of 1 lemon and 1 orange
2 tbsp. orange juice or lemon juice
2-3 tbsp. vegetable oil
1 cup honey
Flour

- Mix eggs and enough flour to make soft dough.
- Roll dough into 1/2 inch wide ropes.
- Cut ropes into 1/2 inch pieces and roll into tiny balls, the size of a dime in circumference.
- Fry dough balls in vegetable oil; do not let them get too brown or burn them.
- Mix honey, zest, juice in a saucepan over low heat until sugar is melted.
- Drain balls and add to warm honey mixture, covering all balls completely
- Arrange balls in a wreath shape on a plate, piling them into layers.
- Optional: Sprinkle with confectionary sugar or colored sprinkles.

Butter Balls

Butter Balls are one of those multi-cultural cookies with an Italian version. Also known as Snowballs, Italian Wedding Cookies, and Mexican Wedding Cookies, they are round and buttery and rolled in powdered sugar. My mother often adds chopped walnuts to hers, but that's optional, as my sister Donna never adds them to hers.

<u>Recipe</u>

1 cup butter, softened
½ cup confectionary sugar
1 tsp. vanilla
2 ½ cups flour
¼ tsp. salt
Optional: ¾ cup chopped walnuts.

- Preheat oven to 400 degrees.
- Mix all ingredients together.
- Roll dough into small balls (smaller than golf balls) and place on ungreased cookie sheets.
- Bake at 400 degrees for 10-12 minutes.
- Remove from oven and roll in confectionary sugar two times while still warm.

Sisters—L to R—Alice, Dahlia and Sue at
Giovanni's farmland in Johnston

THE FIORE WOMEN

Maria Mollo Fiore. My mother speaks of her own mother in saintly tones. Wistfully, solemnly. That's the way I remember my aunts and uncles describing her as well—hushed, looking toward the heavens.

Growing up I believed them without question, never even considering the possibility that my mother's mother could have possessed any bad habits. Nail biter maybe? Short tempered? Chain smoker? No, no and definitely no. "Even though she suffered so much, she never complained," my mother still says. I think about how I whine to my own daughter to lower the TV when I have a mild headache. Far from saintly, I will most likely be recalled in a rant on some therapist's couch one day.

All the Fiore women I've ever known possess a sense of strength and martyrdom that eludes me. I can't even pretend to imitate it.

Auntie Sue's tongue stung with a sharp edge sometimes. If someone in the family gained weight since the last time she saw him or her, she declared it in the bluntest of terms. But likewise, if she had to defend her family to the world outside, she didn't hesitate to battle with the same tenacity. Auntie Sue also possessed the fortitude as a teenager to administer her mother Maria's insulin injections—to stick needles in her mother's arms till they were sore, then her legs, puncturing her like one would a common pincushion. Sue suffered from emphysema as a young woman, and at 26 years-old lost a lung; risky surgery then and now. She demanded my father smoke outside when we visited, shaking her head and clicking her tongue at the sight of his pack of L&M's lying on her kitchen table.

Sue, like the other Fiore sisters, always helped her mother with the cooking. All the recipes were carried down by word of mouth as well as in deed. In adulthood, Sue almost always fed her brothers full meals whenever they visited, even when they had wives and families of their own to cook for them. Heaping platters of thick noodles with gravy and meatballs, or maybe veal cutlets and hearty greens, whatever she had on hand. She presented her meals as a tribute to her brothers and anyone else who entered her home, even those she didn't particularly like.

To Sue's credit, her love of watching people enjoy food and her caution to not lead others into sickness enabled her to often find healthy alternatives to family recipes. A self-trained trailblazer in the art of nutrition, many of her valid suggestions got mistaken for meddling. She despised obesity, especially the heft of her sister Phil. Only now do I appreciate her toughness, watching her mother die of diabetes, stabbing her repeatedly with insulin needles, only to have Maria sneak a plate of cold lasagna in the middle of the night. Sue was ahead of her time, evangelizing healthy eating during the sixties and seventies to our family full of fat and carb-loving ignoramuses. Whole wheat "Hollywood Diet" bread was a favorite of hers; spinach linguine replaced regular yellow. She served "Sugar in the Raw" with coffee, and avoided baking and serving pastry. Any pies that did emerge from her oven oozed with tart, no sugar added fillings Occasionally she would splurge and buy Eskimo Pies or some other type of frozen treat to feed her nieces and nephews when they visited. I vividly recall her direct disapproval of me as a chunky nine-year old, sneaking into her freezer for repeated servings of ice cream pie.

Auntie Sue and Auntie Alice lived together, two spinsters, but not in the sense you'd imagine. They were beautiful, stylish, slim, and fun to be around. I think Alice would have gotten married, but didn't want to leave Sue alone.

Sue criticized most men, especially men who threatened to diminish the spirit of her younger sisters Alice and Dahlia. The tension between Sue and my father sometimes ran thick when we visited "The Girls" in Narragansett.

My mother remembers her two sisters sun-bathing on the Marshall Street porch—teenagers laying out in swimsuits, their skin coated with tanning oil, posing in plain view for the telephone men, street workers, or any other men that happened by. The men gaped in awe. The Girls got a kick of out of teasing them, my mother said with a smile. But neither ever married.

Auntie Alice's heart opened to everyone. She reminded me so much of my mother that I used to think they were twins. Auburn brown wavy hair pulled back, slim Capri pants, house slippers and a silky jersey top—that's how I remember Alice, scuffing around the custom ranch home that she shared with Sue. She was Sue's right hand in the kitchen, also putting her all into preparing food for her family.

I remember lots of rustic browns and ambers in the Girls' house—the epitome of style for the late 60's and early 70's. We kids all enjoyed our visits there in the summer, sleeping over on the enclosed porch, on chaise lounges that were almost as cushy as our beds back home on Greenville Avenue. Their house contained two fireplaces, one with a cool chain-link curtain whose drawstring I continually pulled. Wall to wall carpeting covered all floor space, even the bathrooms and the kitchen. And they had a dishwasher.

Alice worked as a secretary at the sand and gravel business owned and operated by the Fiore brothers. "The Boys" took care of their unmarried sisters, making sure they were housed and clothed luxuriously. When Alice or Sue ventured out, both were always smartly dressed in suits, Alice with round sunglasses like Jackie O, though not quite as large.

Auntie Phil, the oldest Fiore daughter, seemed to best match the image in my mind of my grandmother Maria. Phil looked the like me, round features, curly brown hair. She had a kind smile and a slight gap between her two front teeth. Her nose was small and turned up a bit, a Mollo nose from her mother's side, unlike the larger Fiore nose. Yet, another Fiore sister who could cook herself into a frenzy with the strength of a mule team. Constantly rolling out macaroni dough, cooking and baking to feed her five kids, and anyone else who happened to pass by. Seventeen years older than my mother and enduring more misery than most. By the time I became old enough to have a relationship with Auntie Phil, she was a partial invalid with severe phlebitis in one leg. But she rolled out macaroni dough from her armchair faster and better than anyone I can recall. Whenever I visited she rubbed one or both of my hands with hers, like an intimate handshake and hug combined into one. Love, understanding and compassion all flowed through her hands. All the Fiore women rubbed your hands when they greeted you. I felt Phil's suffering too, through her warm, worn hands. Phil lost her husband to a stroke as a young wife, and her youngest daughter to diabetes 20 years later. I was six at the time, but I remember my cousin Arlene as blond and beautiful, not bloated and sick. She had that same pixie nose that Phil, Sue, my sister Maree and my daughter Julia has. I adored Arlene; she was as kind as her mother to me, and to everyone.

Feeding others. Fiore women were placed upon this earth with this mission. Give them your hungry, your famished, your voracious masses in need of a good home-cooked meal. Even if you're not hungry, just have a little something. Once fed, you must be happy. The tradition in America started with Maria and Giovanni, Mary and John, who perpetually took in multitudes of Italian cousins coming to Rhode Island with no other place to go. According to Dahlia,

"My mother said it was her job to take care of people. And she did. I don't know how she managed to feed so many with nothing, but she did it. Even when she was sick. And she never complained."

To this day my mother is in awe of her own mother's efforts, and her compassion for others above herself. So am I.

Maria received little reward, and little in return for her kindness, but it didn't matter. "Her sisters had so much and all they would bring her was a dozen eggs," my mother told me about her aunts, the Mollo women. "They had all that money and all she got was eggs. And they ate and ate everything she made."

Maria took her commitment to nourish seriously, even wet nursing her cousin's sick babies. She enjoyed the sound of children in her home and all of the Fiore boys and girls would bring their friends over to Marshall Street to enjoy fresh-baked cookies or a nice piping hot doughboy with sugar sprinkled on top.

Food nourishes the soul and the body, makes you feel better and can cure any ailment. Unless of course it kills you, as diabetes killed Maria, Phil, and Arlene.

My mother followed in her mother's and sisters' footsteps. Food made with blood, sweat, tears and love. How many mountains of pastena and butter did she make for me when I didn't feel well? Any kind of macaroni for that matter, as the butter and cheese on it provided me instant remedy from any ailment. My sisters helped themselves to gravy sandwiches by soaking thick slices of Italian bread into my mother's tomato sauce. The meatballs, with their hunks of garlic and fresh basil, *basilico,* tucked inside, were reserved for Sunday dinner. My mother fed the neighborhood kids too, who would stick their faces against our screen door and watch us eat homemade pancakes until invited inside.

My sisters and I can all can cook and bake. We know some of the recipes, but it isn't the same as the Fiores. We all love food; love to eat, sometimes too much. My mother taught us how to make tomato gravy and all kinds of cookies at Christmas time. My sister Donna owns a café and cooks and bakes for a living. She stands as the only one of the four of us who has the stamina and determination of Sue and Phil on a perpetual basis, and experiences the great satisfaction that comes from constantly feeding others.

Even though it is a deeply personal, almost religious experience, giving and preparing food has become only a small slice of who I am, of what I do. It's more of a hobby or a relaxing pastime than a chore that defines me. However small, though, I feel its power over me when duty calls and I take on the nourishment of the masses, aka my family and friends.

As a young girl I loved to cook and bake for others, but marrying a man who considered a bowl of Lucky Charms as a dinner entre caused me to put down my spatula and wave the white apron of surrender some years back. Jeremy has come a long way since our early days together, though there's a bit of room for improvement. And my daughter Julia's taste buds are not yet mature enough to like things like tomato gravy and eggplant. Suffice it to say that neither possesses a palate sophisticated enough to truly appreciate my Italian cooking.

Like the Fiore women before me, my cooking must be appreciated, or alas you have slain me. When I cook, I am tearing off a piece of my own flesh and throwing it into the pot. Other than writing, there is nothing on this earth that gives me more satisfaction than preparing something to be loved and consumed by another human being.

I still make my father squid soup, because I know he loves it, and he loves the way I make it. Tentacles and all, sautéed with onions, butter, olive oil and tomato. When I bring my candied sweet potatoes to my in-laws' each Thanksgiving, I wait and only exhale after receiving some much anticipated compliments. Of course I shrug it off as nothing on the surface. No one knows how much I relish compliments on my cooking, for if you like my cooking, you like me. And if you don't absolutely love my cooking, you reject me and cause me immediate and irreparable emotional damage. That part of my Fiore heritage will never leave me, and I'm happy for it, even though I don't truly understand it.

A good friend of mine was once told by her mother that cooking on Sundays, in her case *Perogies* and *Gołąbki* instead of macaroni and meatballs, was her secret for keeping her sons coming back home each week, as well as giving her grandchildren a reason to enjoy their visits. I believe that's what my grandmother would have done if she could, what Phil and Sue and Alice and my own mother did by making their homes the food hub, the place to go to get a warm meal and a family favorite that cannot be matched in the outside world, inside your belly.

The Girls—L to R—Sue,
Dahlia and Alice at my wedding in 1996

Nursery Rhymes
and Fairy Tales

My mother had a knack for telling bizarre bedtime stories, where animals take on human qualities, while keeping some level of their animal drives and tendencies. In educated circles, this literary device is referred to as Anthropomorphism—the personification of animals, inanimate objects, forces of nature—essentially the non-human. To my mother, and her mother, and back before that, it's a story telling technique used to illustrate human behavior without naming names. From Aesop's Fables, to Mother Goose to Beatrix Potter to Charles M. Schultz, it's a clever way to convey the good and bad sides of human nature while protecting any specific perpetrator identities.

Many of the stories and rhymes my mother told us were hand-me-downs she recalled from those told to her by her own mother.

The story of *Top Off, Half Gone, All Gone* has always been one of my favorites. Night after night I'd beg her to recite it. Here I've added a little punctuation, but little else.

Top Off, Half Gone, All Gone

There once was a Cat and a Mouse who had an arrangement; they were married and had one child, who was ready to be baptized. This family kept a large jar of cream in their cupboard that was not to be touched until the christening.

The Mouse—the wife—had no problem keeping her hands out of the jar of cream, as she knew it was to be saved for this special occasion.

The Cat—the husband—could not stop thinking about the jar of cream and how good it must taste. He convinced himself that all he wanted was a taste, and that he had a right to at least have that.

That night, when his wife wasn't looking, the Cat snuck over to the cupboard and licked the top off of the jar of cream. It was delicious. He smacked his lips and licked his paws he was so happy. All he wanted was a taste.

The next morning his wife asked him, "Have you decided on a name for the baby? In order for the baby to be baptized, he must have a name."

The Cat and Mouse had yet to agree on a name. Once they did, the baptism could take place. The Cat thought that if he stalled, he'd have one more chance at the cream. All he wanted was one more lick. He thought and thought.

"Have you decided on a name?" The wife asked again, growing impatient.

"Top Off."

"Top Off? That's a funny name. Can't you think of anything else?"

"Well, I'll consider it," said the Cat.

That night the cat went back to the cupboard and took some more. The Mouse wondered where he was.

The next morning she said, "I don't like Top Off. Have you come up with any other names?"

"How about Half Gone?" said the cat, softly licking his lips at the thought of the jar of cream he tasted again last night.

"Now that is a very strange name," the Mouse thought.

"I don't like that name at all. How about something else?" she asked.

"I'll consider it," said the Cat.

The following morning, she asked her husband again.

"Have you thought of any more names for the baby? He needs to be baptized."

"All Gone," he said, smacking his lips, quite loudly this time.

"Oh really?" she said. "All gone you say? Well, that sounds like a fine name." She watched her husband carefully. He stopped smacking his lips.

"All gone it is. Now let me see how our jar of cream is doing."

"Oh now I see." She went into the cupboard.

"All gone it is."

And that's just one story.

These nursery rhymes have been carried down from my grandmother to my mother down to us kids, murmured softly as we lay cradled in our loving mothers' arms. It sounds to me like a mix of Pig Latin and Portuguese. Nevertheless, I have done my best below. When I could simply not decipher the words, I looked them up.

My daughter enjoys these rhymes, and finds my mother's Italian hysterically funny. Since she's 12, she finds most things either hysterically funny or totally boring. I'm glad it's not the latter, so as not to hurt her Mimi's feelings. They both enjoy giggling over the bouncy words together.

I cannot recite these from memory. As I was a baby when most of these were given to me, they are only faintly familiar. But they are cute.

La Formica (The Ant)

La formica da mattina a sera le ricerche per cibo e mai fermate
Che va dal campo per campo di ricerca alla ricerca
Senza fine di cerce e cerce e torna indietro fino
Alla notte (candera) alla ricerca di cibo.

Translation:

The ant from morning till night searches for food and never stops
He goes from camp to camp searching, searching
Never ending, search and come back, search and come back
Until night searching for food.

When reciting this next one about the Crazy Rabbit, it's important to count the things that happened to him on one hand. Apparently this adds to the drama. My daughter loves to act this out in a much exaggerated manner, much to my mother's amusement.

The Crazy Rabbit

Ecco la bella piazza
Dove passò il pazzo coniglio è andato turno e turno—
Qualcuno lo ha visto, qualcuno lo ha catturato, qualcuno cucinato lui,
    qualcuno mangiava lui—
E il povero piccolo bambino aveva nessuno.

Translation:

Here is a pretty Plaza
Where passed the crazy rabbit went round and round—
Somebody saw him, somebody caught him, somebody cooked him,
    somebody ate him—
And the poor little baby had none.

Happy times in the backyard on Dover Street. L to R—Tony Testa, Sue Fiore, a family friend of the Testas, Alice Fiore, Dottie Testa, Jenny Testa, and Dahlia. Front and Center is Tony and Jenny's youngest, my Aunt Ann.

LOVE'S OLD SWEET SONG

Music brings order to chaos, entertains and teaches and is a civilized form of self-expression. For the tortured artist, it's a dignified way to rip out a pulsing fistful of your heart and slap it on a plate for an audience who will hopefully devour it with relish. Today, music provides us with many things: a nifty way to pass the time in the car, something to reveal plot and tone at the movies, something to talk loudly over in a restaurant or bar, or, more often than not these days, something to plug into and block out the rest of the world.

Music's ability to create happiness and laughter, to heal during painful times is what Maria Fiore desperately yearned for her rambunctious house full of children to possess. Maria's brother, my mother's Uncle Roger Mollo, lived with the Fiores on Marshall Street, and came from Italy equipped with a vast array of opera records that continually played on the family Victrola, filling the big Victorian home with sweet, strong melodies.

A few of Joe's friends played music, and they often stopped over the house on Marshall Street to play and sing. Those times brought even more life into an already lively house, and brought Maria much healing, joy and contentment as she listened and sang along in the Fiore living room. What Maria wanted was to get her children interested enough to actually play music, to sing well. That was the prize—the badge of sophistication and dignity her children needed in order to become truly civilized. Music provided the key to coping with and ultimately conquering life's sorrows and disappointments.

Maria's attempts were successful to a point. Everyone in the house came to love music; unfortunately music didn't always love them back.

Rolly and Reynolds, the two roughnecks of the brood, didn't include playing musical instruments on their tough guy checklist. When a music professor who lived down the street mysteriously appeared one day with a violin for Rolly, his brothers and sisters busted guts laughing.

To his credit Rolly did take lessons, most likely out of devotion to his mother versus any real love of the instrument. Lessons were 50 cents each in 1934. It was the Depression and money was tight, but Maria Mollo Fiore found a way to stretch what little she had to make this crucial sacrifice, this investment in the future character of her offspring.

Not to be left out and often considering his younger brother as a role model of sorts, Reynolds also took lessons—on the Electric Hawaiian guitar. Although I could hear its twang in my mind, until now I had never seen or heard of an Electric Hawaiian Guitar. I assumed my mother just made up the name, getting steel guitar and electric guitar mixed up. I was wrong. The Electric Hawaiian Guitar is a bona fide musical instrument—played flat on your lap instead of upright. Kind of like an autoharp with a neck. Reynolds, the cool one of the bunch, went for the trendy electric sound instead of the traditional classical tone of Rolly's violin. I can just see the Fox—like a young Dean Martin—his wavy hair and sleepy eyes twanging away in his smooth easy style, feet kicked up with his ol' Hawaiian on his lap. My grandmother must have been floating in paradise to have her two troublemakers making music.

Rolly's artistic refinement lasted four months. For four months both boys played, not together, thankfully. Imagining a duet between them, with an Electric Hawaiian guitar and a violin, brings nothing melodic to mind.

Sadly, the day the music died came much too soon. During an argument that turned a bit physical in nature, the violin, an innocent bystander, became a prop, a weapon, much like a folding chair does in one those TV wrestling matches today. If the Fiore boys had only known what visionaries they would become in the arena of sibling violence. Maria's fragile hopes for a concert violinist in the family shattered into a thousand Stradivarian splinters over

Reynolds' curly mop of hair. She had to pay the music instructor (il spartito maschile) for the damages.

Reynolds played on as a solo act for a little longer, until discovering he preferred to play with girls instead, totally losing interest in his music lessons. So much for culture for the Fiore boys.

Little Dahlia always wanted to play the piano, but was never afforded lessons, not to mention that there was no piano in the house for practice. I'm not sure why she didn't get lessons of some sort. Perhaps the violin/electric Hawaiian guitar experiment was a little too much to bear repeating for her mother? It wasn't as if my mother could do anyone bodily harm with a piano unless she dropped it out of a second floor window. Perhaps there was no more money to spare.

No matter, as there were no more lessons to be had with the instructor down the street. My mother recalls going to her girlfriend Alda's house on the weekends and pretending to play her family's player piano. This may sound slightly pathetic—to pretend that perfect melodies came from your fingers instead of a roll of paper tucked inside the instrument. Or lazy—just play the damn thing! But for little Dahlia, it was her moment of grand expression, and she pictured the crowds cheering her on as her fingers danced along the keyboard, barely touching the ivory but still managing to create the most amazing sounds.

My mother never became a musical protégé. I remember her humming around the house when I was small, especially when she was trying to lull me to sleep if I felt sick (from time to time) or cranky (much more common) with *Sing a Song of Sixpence, Down by the River in the Iddy Biddy Pool,* or *Love's Old Sweet Song.* While the other songs were pretty kid-friendly, *Love's Old Sweet Song* is an old Irish ballad of longing. A bit depressing maybe, but always my favorite. My mother's soft mellow voice rose and fell like a feather floating on a breeze—wistful, calm, with no deliberate direction in mind. She rocked me on our black Boston rocker. I finger traced the Tolle painting that decorated it as she held me.

> *Just a song at twilight, when the lights are low,*
> *And the flick'ring shadows softly come and go,*
> *Tho' the heart be weary, sad the day and long,*
> *Still to us at twilight comes Love's old song,*
> *Comes Love's old sweet song.*

Now that I'm grown and somewhat educated, I'd like to believe her love of this song came from her love of James Joyce, who was known for singing this song at the turn of the 20th century. Alas this is not the case. Her mother used to own a recording of this song, in that wonderful house of music she created. And that song of longing took her right back there.

I think about my mother's life at that time when I was very young. A husband who was rarely home and never changed a diaper, with all of her children almost grown only to have another baby at forty, to do all the chores, all the rearing, all the everything for her own rambunctious brood. I can feel the heaviness of her breath and her heart as she hung on to me, and hung on to herself, rocking us both as she hummed, just to get through the day and the night. Just so we could do it all again the next day.

Family and Friends. L to R—Dahlia, Evelyn Famiglietti, family friend Mike Quintevallo, Nana Familglietti, family friend Anthony Guglielmo, Sue, Alice Familglietti, and Alice Fiore in front of Dover Street.

SKETCH ME IF YOU CAN

Growing up, Dahlia demonstrated many artistic traits, and her love of creation and performance continues to this day. As a young girl she loved imitating both animals and people. When the family had company over she graciously took it upon herself to provide live entertainment. The hallway between the dining room and the kitchen on 63 Marshall Street served not only as a large coat closet, but also as her performance arena. She'd hide between jackets, scarves, and galoshes and begin her set with a little meowing, barking, and bleating. Goats were one of her specialties. She was up for anything really. She had a pair of patent leather Mary Janes upon which her father Giovanni hammered iron taps. The additional clamor only enhanced her performance. Although she wasn't sure if this behavior was typical ten year old girl fare, as long as no one else cared that she was off beat, she had a ball. The laughter emanating from the adjoining rooms made her glow inside. She felt the warmth, like a high, as the glow started inside her gut and radiated out her fingertips—a little girl who was wanted, loved and accepted as the free spirit she longed to be.

In 1936, at age 12, Dahlia won a six month scholarship to the Rhode Island School of Design (RISD), one of the most prestigious art colleges in the country both then and now. Mere blocks from Brown University, on the affluent East Side of Providence, the mix of avante garde and Ivy League was as intriguing then as it is now. One can breathe in the expansion of minds opening to new ideas and modes of expression as you walk down Thayer Street or South Main Street even today.

Brother Joe walked Dahlia to RISD each Saturday morning for her lessons, from Federal Hill to College Hill. They enjoyed the five mile walk together. On those Saturday mornings, the little girl with skinny legs, wearing homemade clothes and hand me downs studied fashion design. Students learned human anatomy, and while this embarrassed the sixth grader, she felt very grown up at the same time. They started by studying then sketching a female model in a swimsuit; the following week a male model in swim trunks.

Most of the other students were older and came from the East Side. Their fathers were not night watchmen at the hat factory, and they hired people to do their gardening instead of tending to roses and tomatoes and grapes in their backyards. Their skin was scrubbed pink and ivory, not dark and olive. The sight of them raised Dahlia's hackles, and she wanted nothing to do with them or their East Side attitudes. She chose to work alone for the most part, her deep-set dark brown eyes soaking up every detail around her, committing to memory all she could about proportion, shading, and the art of adding clothing to those nearly nude models. Her fascination with learning outweighed her desire for friends or popularity. Of course once she was a famous fashion designer those snobs would just be begging to befriend her.

When the scholarship ended, the Fiore family could not afford RISD tuition, so Dahlia left her studies to the older kids from the East Side. No more walks holding Joe's hand through the early morning mist from Marshall Street to the grown up world on the East Side.

Dahlia never let go of her drawing or any of her other artistic pursuits for that matter. While we don't hear too many animal noises these days, drawing and comedy remain part of her repertoire, and when they join together—look out.

My mother loves sketching. She doesn't go to the park or the seaside and sketch the scenery. People are what she loves to sketch—especially people she knows. Unbeknownst to them, for the most part. Her minimalistic style allows her to capture just the right essence of a person's personality and demeanor. All through my childhood I remember her taking out the sketch book, alone sometimes, but usually with my sister Donna, who also loves to draw. They sketched our relatives, and I've been the subject of a sketch or two as well, much to their delight and amusement. It wasn't (and still isn't) meant to be cruel or insulting. Those sketches represent an expressive outlet for my mother, as so many of her other outlets were either taken away or fell away over time with the drudgery of housework and battling offspring. And for us kids, drawing became a way to get closer to my mother, to show her what we could do in her arena.

To witness Donna and my mother's delighted amazement at the resemblances they can conjure wraps you up in a world where my mother is all-knowing and calls the shots. What they will wear and how they will pose. And on those rare occasions, when the artists don't get it right, it's even more amusing. Sometimes they sketch the same person to see who can create the best likeness. Sort of like dueling pencils. I've always loved to draw people, probably to keep up with my mother and my older sister, but also just because creating a human likeness on a page, and watching the two dimensional come alive feeds my spirit with positive energy.

Most delightful of all, my daughter loves to draw, and has been 'sketching' with her Mimi ever since she could hold a crayon. During her formative years one of the first thing she did once arriving at Mimi's is get out the sketch pad and pencils reserved for her, plop next to her on the couch, and start drawing. With the onset of technology, they now spend time creating on my daughter's iPod. My mother conducts her own version of Saturdays at RISD, no swimsuit models thankfully, but as the artistic authority she readily provides Julia with direction. "Now let's draw Papa Al," or "Let's try to draw Mommy …"

Sometimes their sessions become very unorthodox, and in her own Crow style she will tell Julia—"What kind of nose is that? It looks like a stuffed pepper, that's not Mommy's nose." (I am thankful for this clarification.) Or, with adoration she will exclaim "Would you look at that? That is a very remarkable resemblance!" I have watched Julia graduate from making oval versus squiggle faces, to working on shading, perspective, tone, and mimicking her grandmother's style.

My mother and Donna sketch during their work hours at the café my sister runs in Warwick. My mother helps her a few days a week, making her famous turkey chili, and other soups and savories. Once she finishes her cooking for the day, she greets customers, chats with the building staff, fiddles with her Sudoku and crossword puzzles at a little corner table, and sketches while she waits for my father to pick her up. My sister conducts reviews, and any sketches deemed worthy are displayed in special 'employee only' designated areas, providing them both with entertainment and relief as they cook and scrub and serve and start it all over again the next day and the next.

While a pleasant pastime for the sketchers, the sketchees, once they find out what's going on, sometimes grow a little weary of the festivities. We cringe when manila tablets are mentioned at all, even in passing. Those of us who can't draw feel vulnerable. Those of us, who can, want to sharpen our pencils for a caricature duel with the master. Oh yeah, you're going to draw me with a big mole on my chin? Well I'm going to draw you with just the thinnest stubble of a beard a la John Waters. You get the idea. It can get ugly. The sketchpad wields power to those who can master it. God pity those who fall prey to its blasphemous images. And to those who can't laugh at themselves.

A new area of artistic expression that intrigues my mother today is voice recording and video. Well, new to her—these aren't exactly cutting edge media, but my daughter, who tries to bring her electronic game device with her wherever she goes, often drags my mother into her world of distorted recordings and pictures. They sit snuggled together conspiring to wreak audio and video havoc on the rest of the world—or at least the rest of the family. My mother's animal sounds have resurrected, though now she caws like a crow instead of bleating like a goat. They both giggle uncontrollably and my daughter takes their picture together and creates a slide show set to their narrative. Unintentionally they have the same tone, like Greta Garbo with a laugh track behind her. My daughter: "I do love you but I must inform you that I just cut the cheese," to my mother's: "Good Godfrey, you have been so naughty that I must leave this party immediately." It's their special nonsense, and no one understands it but the two of them. My father and I roll our eyes at each other and at the two of them, wondering what the heck they are talking about, grateful for their connection and the laughter therapy that my daughter provides her grandmother. I see a little girl with the deep set brown eyes and the patent leather shoes with taps on them sitting next to a blond, blue eyed athletic goddess-child. My husband grew up on the East Side of Providence and while not part of the wealthy elite, he was immersed in academia by his parents, both college professors, throughout his youth through their long and distinguished careers. I can't help but think how nice it is that the dark little girl from Marshall Street can now make friends with the East Side kids after all, and that they are surprisingly similar in so many ways.

Bridgham Junior High 9th Grade Graduation.
Dahlia is in the 4th row up, 5th girl in.

SCHOOL DAYS

My mother kept notes about her school days, and is proud of her accomplishments, though they were short-lived.

"I started school late. I was seven when I started kindergarten, with Miss Flynn. When I was six I dropped the iron on my leg and burnt it so bad that I had to miss a year of school. I was trying to help my mother and iron the clothes."

"I remember Miss Flynn—she was so pretty and probably in her thirties. And so patient. She never yelled or made us not want to participate, and she always picked me to erase the board because I never spoke out and always behaved."

"I had Mrs. Gorman for first grade. She was older and very different from Mrs. Flynn—some kids tried her patience. I tried to do what I was told."

"Second Grade was Miss O'Donnell. She taught us quite a bit about shopping and money, how to buy, and I thought that was neat. All I ever knew was how to buy candy whenever I had some pennies. She had us build a big cardboard store. It took up the back of the classroom, and she would nominate one of us to manage it. We made groceries out of cardboard and put prices on them. What we learned came in handy when my mother asked me to go to the grocery store later.

"At the end of third grade I left Almy Street School and started at Kenyon Street. This school was huge—500 kids from all over the city, not just the familiar faces from Almy Street. We began our walk to school at seven in the morning from Marshall Street to get to Broadway by 7:30. Once we got to the school grounds we'd play tag or just gab until the start of school at 8. We entered the building two by two, a line of boys and a line of girls.

"Mrs. Burdick was a large woman principal and reminded me of a bull dog, even the boys behaved around her as she took no nonsense. Every month she came to our classroom to check on our progress. She liked me, and asked me to do a mural after seeing my drawings. Michael Guerra was a boy in my grade who was a fantastic drawer. We worked together on a 'Beauty and the Beast' mural that graced the principal's office wall.

"I hated to leave that school at the end of sixth grade—to Brigham Junior High with more than 1,000 kids. That's when I decided I would like to be an art teacher. But once I got through with Junior High things began to change. I know my brother Joe and my mother wanted me to go to college, but I couldn't see how they could pay for it.

"But I enjoyed Junior High. There was a movie theatre at the school. It was five cents a show. The last movie I remember seeing there was 'The Grapes of Wrath.'

"Then there was Amateur Day in the auditorium. I sang a song called 'The Pink Police Gazette.' I got some applause, but a few teachers had raised eyebrows. Sue and Alice would sing all these songs and bought song sheets, so I took it from them. 'The pretty young brunette on the pink police gazette…'

"In 1940, when I was 15, we did an operetta. I played the part as a southern belle. My sisters Sue and Alice bought me a beautiful off shoulder blue and white gown. I wore that gown to a waltz contest too. I went with Tony Guglielmo, my brother Roland's friend. He was a spiffy dresser and smelled nice. His father was a furrier and his mother was always talking about wedding bells. We won, and I got a mahogany jewelry box with the *year engraved on it. I didn't like Tony, but Roland didn't want other boys to go out with me.*

"I wore that blue and white gown to a football dance too. Joe didn't care for the off shoulders. So I pulled it up before I left the house—and pulled it back down when I got there."

"I got asked to the prom in ninth grade by Tony DiTorro. He was so handsome, and his family had money. When I told my brothers, they said no; you are going with Tony Guglielmo. Tony DiTorro was very sad when I told him I had to go with my brother's friend."

That's where most of the school memories end. My mother quit school when she was 17 years old. She had been taking secretarial courses going into 11th grade, and doing very well. But after her mother died, she found it difficult to concentrate. Her grades were always good; but now, after losing Maria that August, she became mixed up. I always knew she quit, but never asked her why. I assumed the stress of losing her mother was too much. We talked about it on the phone one night.

"My mother always wanted to see my report cards, even though she couldn't understand much English. My mother's dying words to my brother Joe were 'Take care of Dahlia. Make sure she stays in school.' That promise wasn't kept.

"When I told my counselor at high school that I was leaving, he said I could always come back. I told him I would think about it, but I knew I wasn't coming back. In those days, we didn't have counselors to talk to about how you felt. I really think I was depressed, but who knew what depression was in those days? Either you were nuts or you weren't."

Towards the end of Maria's life, as she became the family's center of attention and care, the patient, Dahlia looked on in the background helplessly.

There was mutual love, adoration, respect. Maria held on for Dahlia's sake, through the hospitalizations back and forth. Maria tried to remedy the pain by going to her bedroom and praying. She didn't want to leave anyone behind, mostly Dahlia, who was so young. But she could hang on no longer as the sugar ate through her body, replacing her blood with syrup. The mortician who embalmed Maria, a family friend, told them how the blood was all brown and thick, not resembling blood at all. That's what the sugar did.

In her early childhood Dahlia found it easy to get her mother's attention. And if her mother wasn't around there was always Phil and her other siblings to watch over her, to keep her happy, loved and entertained.

Becoming a teenager changed everything for Dahlia. She looked grown up, but was still a little tap dancing girl inside who wanted her family to laugh. She wanted her mother to laugh and share secrets, but how can you share secrets with someone in a sugar coma? Energy dwindling, and getting worse each day, with no time to focus on Dahlia. And sisters aren't mothers no matter how good the intention. Everyone was losing Maria, but the devastation that everyone felt couldn't match the isolation that Dahlia the teenager felt. She needed a mother's ear and advice most, with soothing assurances that everything will be okay. There was none of that. Dahlia lost out.

Meeting my father was the first option presented to Dahlia after her mother's death. The Testas were stable family with a strong mother, making decisions, taking charge, making sure the rules were set and followed. So different from the life she knew.

Dahlia and Alice strike a pose in Newport, RI

THE PICTURE MAN

Sometimes it's way too easy for me to hold my own pity party, or beat myself up because I don't think I'm doing enough—for my family, my friends, my employer, my community. I can really lay it on myself heavily.

But now that I understand my mother's world better, I cannot help but think about her growing up, and all she missed.

What matters most to her now is that for all of the birthday cakes, milestones and ritual celebrations she may have missed, she received love, security and adoration from her parents, her brothers and her sisters in tenfold.

So now instead of reflecting on my own shortcomings as Super Mom, Homemaker of the Millennium, and Chairperson of the Perfect Wife Club, I remind myself of how intensely I love my family, how many opportunities my daughter has and will have, how grateful I am to have a husband who is loving, compassionate, consistent and a rock for me to lean on, and all the wonderful friends that I admire so much.

Oh yeah, and Zingarella, my tabby cat who has been snuggling up next to me each night for over sixteen years, and Trudy, our Beagle, who greets me like I've been gone for centuries when I've just gone downstairs to throw a load of whites in the wash. Happiness is definitely a warm puppy—or a cuddling cat.

And now, after writing down my mother's stories, I will think of little Dahlia chasing the Picture Man. She had the right idea because sometimes, really most times, we have to create our own opportunities for happiness.

My mother's First Holy Communion came and went without celebration. She does not remember ever blowing out her birthday candles as a child.

Having a sick mother, with so many unexpected relapses, dampened many celebrations. Sometimes Dahlia came home from school to find her brother Joe had driven Maria to Roger Williams Hospital due to a sugar coma. Maria usually came back home within a few days, but Dahlia, as the youngest, often felt confused and lost.

Maria Mollo Fiore's formal diagnosis of diabetes, commonly known to the family at the time just as Sugar, came in 1931. She suffered from gestational diabetes when pregnant with Dahlia, but for seven years she went on, suffering with constant thirst and urination, spastic diarrhea as her body rejected each meal, exhaustion, and fits of labored, gasping breathing, without treatment. Finally, a loss of consciousness led to the diagnosis.

Insulin gained some level of recognition as a treatment in the 1930s, but most diabetics at the time were treated with cruelly restrictive diets that could send a person's system into shock with even the slightest infraction. Diabetics crave sugar, crave carbohydrates, and crave thick crusty bread and gooey lasagna, zeppole gorged with custard cream or frosting, and anything else essentially deadly to their vascular systems. So Maria ate, and endured the insulin needles administered by her daughter Sue, the only one with the strength to bear injecting her mother's arms, then legs, full of holes several times a day. Maria endured the humiliation of heating her urine on the stove every day, dropping a few drops of some magic blue potion into her pee to determine her blood sugar level. My mother remembers carrying home bottles of this mysterious blue liquid from the drug store, but she doesn't remember the contents. Bright orange meant high blood sugar. My mother recalls watching the liquid and hoping it would remain blue, so her mother could stay safe—for the time being.

The Fiore diet, like most Italian diets of the time, included a multitude of rich carbohydrates, like home-made pastas, breads and pastries. Maria adored home-made macaroni, and her wifely and motherly rituals included constantly conjuring the thick, flat noodles, rich in eggs and flour to feed her family. She rolled the dough by hand, transforming elastic stickiness into docile, smooth slabs with nothing more than a rolling pin, cupfuls of flour and brute strength. She folded the slabs into rolls, and then sliced them into ribbons. The noodles got rolled in cornmeal and set it to dry on linen sheets laid on the kitchen table. The Fiore girls helped. The process required strength and stamina and hours of mixing and rolling to get the right consistency.

Maria enjoyed the process and the product, whether freshly boiled and topped with sharp, sweet tomato gravy at supper, cold out of the fridge for breakfast, or as a snack when the need drove her in the middle of the night. Her family's attempts to dissuade her failed—most of them possessed kindly natures not meant for confrontation. Once again it was Sue who possessed the stamina to confront, yelling at Maria in a desperate attempt to control her mother's urges. Desperate to avoid another day of needles and sores and scars. But the disease always won, craving the carbs, feeding off them while tearing through Maria's body, leading her to an early death. That she lived as long as she did during those times amazes me.

Although she didn't quite understand the disease, Dahlia did try to help out during her mother's absences. She tried to iron, with mixed results, and the way she folded the laundry always made her mother smile upon her return home.

My mother remembers her brothers and sisters always appearing preoccupied during Maria's relapses, working mostly, while my mother anxiously anticipated the coming of birthdays, graduations, and other holidays. She assumed they weren't interested in such celebrations, or that they had better things to do with their time. Only Phil. Phil always tried to amuse her little sister, to make sure there was something fun to distract her, whether it was shopping or just helping in the kitchen. Dahlia spent many of these times with her sister Phil and her family. She often thought of Phil as her second mother, her nieces and nephews as little brothers and sisters she could adore and care for. Phil treated her little sister like one of her own brood. She sought to make Dahlia feel special and adored, especially when their mother was in the hospital, or at home but totally depleted of strength.

Dahlia tried to make sense of the fact that she possessed no First Communion pictures or gifts. Today she holds no fond memories of birthday games at home or in the backyard with her family or schoolmates. At the time, she didn't understand why more wasn't made of special occasions, and she did not like being denied these rites of passage. So, when the opportunity presented itself, little Zat took it upon herself to make things happen.

What I love best about my mother's stories is that there's always some character with a specific role to play passing through her old neighborhood at just the right moment. Like actors in a play, someone enters stage right and moves the scene forward with perfect timing. Like the Rag Man, who traveled up and down the street in a horse-drawn cart to take old cloth, (and naughty little children, thought Dahlia). Or the music instructor who seems to arrive just as music lessons are needed. And the photographer, known simply as the Picture Man. The Picture Man lost a leg during World War I and passed through the neighborhood every so often with his tripod, making his living by offering to take pictures for a quarter or 50 cents. Today such solicitations sound a bit perverse, but not so in 1931.

One day, shortly after Dahlia's First Communion, she looked out the living room window to find the Picture Man hobbling down Marshall Street. She raced into her bedroom and threw on her first communion dress and veil, trying as well as any seven-year-old to preserve every fashion detail of the holy day. She stole fifty cents from her mother's purse and ran outside to get her picture taken. Her pride in that picture, in her self-commemoration of her special day, gave her the courage to continue this fine art of self-promotion when necessary.

Like the time her mother had sewn a beautiful light brown satin dress with delicate ruffles on the skirt. Maria joked with her little olive-skinned girl. "It's the same color as you!" she told her warmly.

Again, the Picture Man presented himself just in time to capture the beauty of that creamy brown taffeta, and how it complemented my mother's long brown hair and big brown eyes.

I wish we still had those pictures, but they are long gone. Lost between moves and family members scrambling between themselves to hold on to memories as their parents passed on.

Maria endured regular trips to the hospital, as the sugar comas became more frequent. Finally, with family finances dwindling, she decided to give up the treatments. They just didn't have the money. I'm sure she realized this meant a sure death in a short period of time. Dahlia, a teenager now, but still the youngest, still the baby, understood what this meant too. She didn't need to live with Phil now, the way that she did when she was seven. Maria, tired and ravaged, readied herself to let go.

My mother vividly remembers her mother's last day—August 3, 1941. And the night before. The torture that breathing became for Maria, as diabetes left untreated eventually suffocates its victims. The family doctor, on his way out from what would be his final visit, told my grandfather Giovanni it would be soon. No matter how many shots of insulin Sue or the doctor stuck into her, she only had days, maybe hours.

Maria battled for air that night, frantically trying to hold on. From my mother's bed she heard the loud gasps through the wall, and the gaps in time between each one. Dahlia, and all the children, felt helpless, so little could be done at this point. Giovanni stayed by his wife's side and stroked her hair, trying to comfort her as best he could.

Maria battled through that night and through much of the next day. A white pigeon landed on her bedroom window ledge and, looking in, began cooing. Someone later told my mother that an angel landed there to take Maria away to heaven. The clock struck three, and at exactly 3 o'clock that afternoon, Maria let go. On her 38th wedding anniversary, August 3, 1941, yet another milestone that would not be celebrated. Her final words were to her son Joe, "Take care of Dahlia." My mother had just turned seventeen.

My grandmother's body lay embalmed in the house for five days. In those days, wakes were held in actual family parlors, not funeral parlors, with family and friends passing in and out, crying, laughing, eating, cooking, while the body lay there.

Those nights held a strange combination of eeriness and comfort for Dahlia. She found it difficult to sleep with her mother lying dead in the living room, but comforted by having her there instead of buried in the ground. And the sadness. Her own of course, but as she watched her father each night, after everyone left, as he sat next to his wife for hours, stroking her hair, she realized the depth of his loneliness, his helplessness, and she worried.

My mother's life of laughter and indulgence never returned. Of course the family did laugh again in time, and they still protected Dahlia, but not in the same way. At seventeen she lost her mother and she met my father. Four years later, they would marry. Her life changed forever.

I am thankful my mother didn't suffer any major physical ailments during my childhood. Once in a while she threw her back out and had to lie still in bed. I cannot remember anyone really waiting on her, the way she cared for us if we had a cold or an earache or anything worth moaning about. I remember one time when I was around seven or eight and she had to go in for a D and C (Dilation and Curettage). She was gone one night that seemed like forever. I felt lost without her, even though I had two sisters a brother and a father at home to care for me. I remember her bringing me back a checker set from the hospital gift store, like some kind of souvenir from a trip to Cape Cod. She didn't bring gifts back for anyone else, and I felt special, though a bit puzzled. Many years later I understand the importance of that gift. She wanted to make sure I knew, as her youngest and not really understanding, that even if she was away, our connection remained.

I am forever grateful and blessed to have had my mother around and healthy for every milestone, every celebration, and every photo opportunity.

Holy Ghost Church on Federal Hill on May 6, 1946. Not only were my parents married there, but also my grandparents Maria and Giovanni Fiore, and my Aunt Phil and Uncle Emilio Tanzi.

NICKELS, DIMES, QUARTERS AND BREAD

T he marriage of Philomena Fiore and Emilio Tanzi took place on Thanksgiving Day 1929, with my then five-year-old mother as flower girl. Just as my grandparents did, Phil and Emilio also married in Holy Ghost Church, with a huge reception afterwards at Roger Williams Park Casino. Phil, along with my mother's Aunt Clara, helped Maria with the cooking required for the nearly 200 guests. A band comprised of Joe's friends played sax, piano, clarinet and trumpet while everyone ate, drank and danced.

The Casino, built at the end of the nineteenth century, serves today as a historical landmark in Providence. People still rent it for up-scale weddings, charity events and galas. I can only imagine how impressive it must have been then for Phil and Emilio's family and friends to dine in the majestic structure when it was nearly new—domed 20 foot ceilings, adorned on the outside by powerful Greek columns, overlooking the water, with a bandstand extending out over Roosevelt Lake. I've passed by so many times on the way to the Roger Williams Park Zoo, or the Carousel, that I've taken its majestic stature for granted.

Renting the casino meant use of the ballroom, tables and chairs, and a kitchen. The older ladies in the family worked the kitchen, warming and serving the food. The menu included what is known as Italian Wedding Soup today—chicken soup with pasta, escarole and tiny meatballs added; also thick homemade noodles in tomato gravy with meatballs and sausage; roasted chicken and potatoes, garnished with fried wild mushrooms and chopped onions; and since it was Thanksgiving Day, turkey, sweet potatoes and stuffing. All of the food was prepared at home, then transported via a few Buicks owned by relatives and friends, and Joe's Model T. Five miles back and forth from Marshall Street to the Elmwood section of Providence.

And there was more. In addition to wedding cake, dessert included all kinds of home-made pastry—bushel baskets filled with crispy wandies— paper-thin fried strips of dough tied in loose knots and sprinkled with powdered sugar; platters of delicate pastry slices filled with prunes, apricots, and figs, moist round almond cookies and crunchy biscotti. Dishes of pastel-colored, whiskey-filled Jordan almonds decorated each table.

To drink—Giovanni's thick, rich homemade wine by the case, along with cases of whiskey and beer. The children drank soda mostly. Their elders also allowed them a mix of wine and orange soda. Kids ran around, happy and sweating in their best clothes, exhilarated by a sugar and diluted alcohol buzz. Many years later, I experienced the same tradition— and sensation—during the holidays. Lots of rich wine sloshing around in adult glasses while we kids got our precious servings diluted with orange soda. That Italian tradition died out, though, as giving children wine at the table didn't exactly fit the wholesome American image we longed to attain.

The bridal party consisted of four bridesmaids—Angie, a tenant from downstairs, Florence from across the street, Clara, not Aunt Clara but a friend of Alice, and someone else my mother can't remember. Sue was maid of honor. Ushers included family friends—Fred, also known as Gib, who owned a hardware store on Atwells Avenue, Cole, Paul, and of course their friend Joe

Beans—of which there must be a minimum of one in every Italian story. Brother Joe was the best man.

Dahlia, the flower girl, transformed into a movie star that day. She flounced about glamorously in pale pink chiffon, ruffles swaying above her pink knee socks and black patent leather shoes. At the church she carried a basket filled with rose petals, but decided to take a sprint down the aisle rather than the agreed upon dignified stroll. Her straight dark hair was meticulously curled that day, the bridesmaids spending the morning fawning over her as if she were a little doll. And that's what she believed she was.

I never met my Uncle Emilio. My mother remembers his white linen suits and his reddish brown hair. He was tall and strong, and had a sweet, baby face with cupid lips and a thin nose.

My Grandmother Maria liked Emilio. He came from her village in Italy, and he knew her people. They often sat together in the kitchen, talking Italian, peeling chestnuts together for stuffing or completing some other cooking chore, for Emilio loved to cook.

Phil adored Emilio—everyone in the family loved Emilio—except Sister Sue. According to my mother, Sue resented Phil marrying before she did, and it didn't matter that Phil was the eldest.

Sue believed her own refinement, looks and fashion sense were superior to Phil's—and she was probably right. Phil was heavy-set and rounder in the face, not interested in clothes, but easy to love—always laughing and good-natured. And patient with everyone, especially her little sister Dahlia, who she cared for as if she were her own daughter.

My mother often refers to Phil as her second mother, because of all the time she spent living with her and Emilio. Phil and Emilio's five children, Rudy, Lola, Marie, Ronnie and Arlene, felt more like her siblings than nieces and nephews, and gave her the chance to be a big sister—a role she took great pride in.

Phil and Emilio honeymooned in Boston, and then settled there, while Emilio worked a steel mill job nearby. Six months later they took a bus trip Providence for a visit, and took Dahlia back to live with them in their rented cottage in Hyde Park.

My mother does not remember a lot about the area except that they lived near a walkover bridge near the river (Turtle Pond, perhaps?). She lived with them for a few months during one of Maria's extended illnesses. At night they would take walks and go for ice cream. They spent many afternoons window shopping, and planning their eventual move back to Providence.

As Emilio's job in Boston provided good steady work, the couple was bound to stay there until he could find something better back home. Eventually Dahlia and the Tanzis returned to Providence, Emilio getting a job working in Scialo's bakery on Federal Hill baking bread. Bridesmaid Angela and her family moved out from downstairs and Phil and Emilio moved into the first floor on Marshall Street. Dahlia lived in both places and enjoyed the convenience of having her second mother just a floor away. Emilio brought home boxes of pastry and bread each night from Scialo's. Maria ate them along with the rest of the family, and her diabetes worsened.

Emilio saved quite a bit of money in Italy before he moved to Providence. He kept pristine records and was very organized, unlike his wife Phil, who was a gifted cook, sweet, hardworking, but not the least bit interested in numbers or order of any kind. As a young girl, Maria would tell her daughter; "Dress up, take a shower first thing when you get up. Have discipline so you can do what you need to do." Phil never listened to her mother and became sloppier as the years went on, sloppier and heavier and less disciplined. But always kind and generous, not to mention strong as a bull. She could roll linguini so fast it could make your head spin.

Phil and Emilio started out well together in Providence, and furnished the first floor of Marshall Street in grand style; mahogany, marble and crystal from Boston considered quite elaborate by the family's standards. Phil and Emilio bought an ivory-colored Boston rocker for Dahlia that was just her size. Dahlia spent many days basking in the sun parlor on the second floor, and then carrying her chair downstairs for her visits with the Tanzis'.

Rudolph Rocco Tanzi—nicknamed Sonny—was born on Marshall Street when my mother was seven years old. She remembers the day Dr. DiSanto came to the house with a big satchel. He pointed to it and told her the baby was right in there. Later on that day she heard the baby crying, so she believed him.

Sonny became the pride of the whole Fiore family. The first grandchild, first grandson, with lush brown curls and a cherub face. My mother beamed with pride at becoming an aunt. She loved taking him for walks up and down Marshall Street, all by herself with Sonny in the carriage first, and later in a stroller as he grew. Phil would take them both window shopping.

"Which toys do you like the best?" she'd ask them both. My mother remembers Rudy pointing to an expensive toy organ being played by a stuffed monkey. Phil bought it for him. Whenever Dahlia asked for anything, Phil would find some way to get it for her. Once when she wanted roller skates but her brother Joe said no, that only 'Toughies' had roller skates, Phil got them for her anyway, thus beginning my mother's roller skating lessons on the linoleum hallway of Marshall Street, much to brother Joe's dismay.

Phil loved her children too much to ever say no to them. Even Maria spoiled them, much more than she ever spoiled my mother, as she is quick to tell me 80 years later.

Many of Dahlia's treasures paid the price of love. "Let them have it," Maria told her wearily when my mother fought to keep her porcelain tea set out of their clutches. Unfortunately the Tanzi kids' idea of a tea party was chucking cups and saucers at one another, leaving Dahlia's tea set in a pile of shards and rubble. Her beloved platinum wood rocker didn't make it either, becoming part of the carnage and havoc set forth by her little nieces and nephews.

The Tanzi family eventually bought a bakery on Federal Hill in 1946— with Emilio doing most of the baking while Phil ran the front and dealt with the customers. They lived on top of the bakery with their five children. Emilio had high blood pressure—my mother remembers how his light-skinned face turned beet red after a day in the kitchen, and how he constantly mopped his brow with sweat. And while their bakery was very tidy, organized and disciplined thanks to Emilio, the upstairs, Phil's responsibility, lacked the same clarity and order.

The fine furnishings still stood sturdy and determined, but definitely scarred by battle. The children literally destroyed everything they got their hands on, in a whirling dervish much like the Tasmanian Devil ripping through aardvarks, bats, beetles, buffalo, old gnus, and the like.

My parents lived with the Tanzis in 1950, on the third floor above the bakery. My sister Maree was around three and my mother was pregnant with my brother Al. My parents loved them dearly, but Phil's slovenliness proved more than my mother could bear. Rats ran through the walls at night, drawn to the flour from the bakery, and the Tanzi kids threw all kinds of stuff on the stairs as bait—nickels, dimes, quarters, bread. If you needed spare change all you had to do was open the door and look down. My mother waited at night in terror, imagining the rats gnawing through the walls, crawling up the steel-tipped steps, devouring her little girl. My parents moved as soon as they could afford it.

It was during the summer of 1950 when Emilio finally went to the doctors. He'd been feeling dizzy a lot, with recurring headaches that hung on for days.

His doctor, Dr. Bellino, treated all of our family, including my mother. One day, the doctor told my mother that Emilio's organs were beginning to give out. His cholesterol and blood pressure were sky-high. There was nothing more to be done. My mother was afraid to tell Phil. My guess is that the doctor wanted someone to know, to be prepared. Emilio probably never told Phil. He didn't want her to worry.

Shortly thereafter Emilio ended up in the Rhode Island hospital with a bad headache. Unaware her husband lay sick in a hospital bed, Phil started down the steel-tipped stairway to the bakery. My mother heard the crack and ran to the top of the stairs from the third floor. She couldn't bear to look, and so Phil's daughter Lola, 16 at the time, went down and wrapped her mother's head in a towel as blood spewed everywhere. My Uncle Danny took Phil to the hospital where she lay bleeding and delirious while her husband, in the same hospital on the same day, died of a brain hemorrhage.

A few days later, on the day of Emilio's funeral, Phil came home from the hospital with a stitched scalp. It was then that she was told that her husband died and would be buried that day.

My mother took care of all of the children on the day of the funeral—Joe's kids MaryAnn and Johnny, the five Tanzi kids, and my sister Maree at the house on Federal Hill. A German Shepard that my uncles used as a watch dog at their concrete plant named Dog-O was let into the yard that day. Dog-O wanted inside and petrified my pregnant mother and the children. He clawed the door with great strength. And when the door began to buckle, my mother got the children up to the roof and stayed there until everyone came home from the burial. Dog-O clawed the door almost to shreds. I'm thinking he smelled the rats or the bread.

After that, the fate of bakery was in limbo. A family friend named Mondo helped them for a while, but without someone like Emilio to bake the bread every day, the business failed and my Auntie Phil lost everything else that mattered. Sonny died of a brain hemorrhage thirty or so years later, and her youngest son Ronnie died of a brain hemorrhage ten years after that. Phil became sick with diabetes, as did her youngest daughter Arlene who died at 26 in 1970. Marie died a few years ago of an infection during surgery. Only Lola remains, with her father's face and her mother's strength.

For all Phil endured, her disposition was almost always pleasant. As a child, I don't remember her ever acting cross or angry with anyone, though I'm sure she had plenty of reason to. At her house on White Drive, she always greeted us from her huge leather chair, one leg purple and withered at the calf with phlebitis. She'd smile as each of us approached her, holding our hands in hers, rubbing our fingers and smiling, so very glad to see us, always telling us how good we looked as we leaned down to kiss her face. So easy to love.

Dahlia and Alphonse's engagement portrait

WHEN DAHLIA MET ALPHONSE

Dad's kind of pasty today, and he looks weary, sitting back in his recliner, a blanket over his legs, and his left arm in a brace. His face still a bit swollen with fluid, he's recovering from pneumonia and a stress fracture to his left wrist. He struggles to clear the phlegm when he tries to speak. I feel like a nag as I hand him more water.

I brought them pastry today, Eccles cakes and some apple turnovers. He adores sweets. My mother looks on with a scowl. "He doesn't need that junk," as she peeks into the box to see what she likes. "What's an Ecco cake anyway?" as she takes the large round cookie filled with raisins and berries and bites. The sugar-coating crunches in her mouth. "Mmmm, not bad," she says with a mouthful and nods.

I curl up on their love seat in their living room and wait for the Crow to get settled in her perch, across from me on the couch. I'm relaxed on the outside, carefully braced for chaos inside. Getting my parents to agree upon the details of anything, whether it's what my sister said on the phone an hour ago, what the doctor told my mother about her blood pressure yesterday, or what my father had for breakfast this morning. These recent facts are tough enough. How will we travel back over 70 years to 1941 together and gain some semblance of a story about their first meeting? I need to know what happened from 1941 to 1947. Six years that set the stage.

In those six years—July 1941 to September 1947—the entire world seemed to come of age. Pearl Harbor, World War II, the Bomb, all changed the planet, the nation, and its neighborhoods for all time forward. America changed from naïve, innocent and brave, to weary, worn and questioning the meaning of victory—of happiness.

Dahlia's life totally changed too, faster than she ever could have ever imagined.

She turned 17 in July of 1941, and lost her mother to diabetes one month later. Dahlia spent the next year floating around, like a spirit in limbo, cold and lost without Maria's warmth, her love, her protection.

Then the turning point, October 1942, when Dahlia Lydia Fiore met Alphonse Robert Testa. An occasion my mother describes as, "Very odd."

After her mother died, Dahlia left Mount Pleasant High School without graduating. She got a job in the shipping room at Uncas Manufacturing in Providence. Among her co-workers were the three Famiglietti sisters, Alice, Nanna, and Evelyn. Alice Famiglietti, short, stocky and sweet, got immense joy out of doing good deeds for others, whether they wanted them done or not. She pressed Dahlia hard, trying to convince her to meet her cousin Alphonse. At 21, Al had received his call for service and was set to leave in two weeks, on November 2. Alice Famiglietti decided Al needed a nice girlfriend to write letters to—and get letters from. How could he go off to war to who knows where—well, eventually who knows where, initially Abilene Texas—and have no one at home pining, worrying and dreaming of him each night?

And who more intriguing than Dahlia Fiore? Compared to the Testas, Dahlia looked downright exotic with dark, deep set eyes, rich mahogany shoulder length hair, and olive skin. That, along with her petite stature and mischievous, dry sense of humor couldn't be more of a contrast for Alphonse—tall, lanky, blonde, blue-eyed, almost Arian-looking. His determination and intensity more than compensated for his pale appearance.

"He looked like a big grey tom cat, in that tweed jacket. I liked blondes with blue eyes." My mother recalled with a grin. I looked over at the white-haired 91 year old man with the swollen ankles propped up in the recliner. Not exactly a prowling alley cat, except for his piercing blue eyes. Even through his thick progressive lenses, they still bring intrigue to his otherwise milk toast appearance.

I do not know what prompted cousin Alice to match these two up, except that neither of them happened to be attached to anyone else. Perhaps she had the keen insight to sense the fragile shyness they shared, hesitant to put themselves out there, looking, but not quite hard enough for that perfect someone to love.

My father's version: he was an innocent victim of circumstance. He went to his uncle Rocco Famiglietti's in search of gasoline ration stamps. Not his uncle Rocco DeLuca's, but his uncle Rocco Famiglietti. Only an Italian in Providence could possibly have two Uncle Roccos.

Rocco Famiglietti, Alice Famiglietti's father, also had a son, Eddie, who went off to the South Pacific in October 1941, leaving his car behind. Thus the extra gas stamps that my father longed for. He needed the gas for his own car, a 1935 Ford V8.

"I was writing letters to Eddie, too," my mother chimed in. "He was so nice. Alice wanted me to be Eddie's girlfriend first. But I didn't want a boyfriend."

"Who else were you writing to?" I said. "The whole neighborhood?"

"We all wrote to lots of boys in the service," my mother explained with pride. "Poor Eddie ended up dying during Pearl Harbor, though."

"No, no, no. He was in the South Pacific," my father said.

"Well, where do you think Pearl Harbor was?"

"I know that. Pearl Harbor is in Hawaii. He was there and …"

"…and he died at the bombing of Pearl Harbor. I said that."

They went, back and forth, stressing each syllable as if the other suffered from dementia.

"I think we're all saying the same thing here," I tried to mediate. "Dad, then what happened?" He cleared his phlegm and continued.

Alice decided to strike. She started talking about a "nice little girl who works with us. You should meet her. She stands out there at the gate at lunch every day. Why don't you take a drive by and take a look?" He told Alice that if she looked like something he wanted, he would stop, and if not, he would just keep going. So Alice, and later Evelyn, conspired with my father to take a look at Dahlia at the Uncas gate. The other Famiglietti sister, Nanna, short for Antoinette, did not involve herself with this intrigue. She hung out with Dahlia's sister Alice. They all worked together at Uncas, which I thought was charming. Of course it's a well known historical fact that lots of Italian Americans worked at Uncas Manufacturing. But these old, mostly deceased people who I always assumed were forced to come together through my parents' marriage, were really all young friends of their own accord. Working together, socializing. They all liked each other.

On that fateful day, no one remembers the exact date, but one day in October, Evelyn, Alice and Dahlia were out talking at the Uncas gate. Al drove by in his Ford V8.

"I was 18. I said okay, I'm willing to take a look at him. Alice said that he's going to go by and for me to stay near the Uncas fence. If he thinks you're good looking he'll stop and if you're not, he'll keep going."

"What? Say that again?" I really thought I heard wrong. My mother willingly posed outside against a wrought-iron fence, and waited for some strange man to drive by, look at her, and decide if she was worthy of his company based solely on her looks? Yes, I know it was 1942, a time when the sexes were less than equal, when the streets of Providence were a safe place to stand on display waiting for men to check you out. But really?

I had not misunderstood.

I suppose I had always wanted to believe my parents met in some magical way—some mysterious, adventurous, dramatic fashion. Perhaps love at first sight, but a drive by? I suppose it is unique, and cute. Perhaps they both held their breath with excitement and the adrenaline rush at the potential of being the approver and the approved. And I'm proud of my mother, that she held sufficient confidence in her beauty to endure this "evaluation" from a stranger. And did my father even realize for one moment the devastation any woman would have suffered if he kept on driving, rejecting her in the broad daylight of Niantic Avenue? No, because she wasn't supposed to know.

"I knew—didn't I? Alice told me about you. Didn't she? I wasn't supposed to know but I think I knew."

"He stopped, and we all went to the Oaks and got sodas and got to know each other."

He asked her to the movies. The Glenn Miller band was playing the song they would dance to at their wedding, *At Last.*

"He said, 'My mother is having a going away party and I'd like for you to come.' Then the next night we went on a date to the High Hat. The High Hat was a fancy and expensive restaurant. I was 18 and could not take a drink. I was told very clearly by my brothers that I could not take a drink. So I had a ginger ale. He was 21, and he had a rum coke."

While Al charged full steam ahead with the courtship, Dahlia dragged her heels into the ground, attempting to slow his momentum.

"I didn't want to go steady with anyone. I never thought I would be getting married for a long time—because I wanted to be a school teacher. But that dream floated away because I left school at 17 and never went back."

Al tried his best to sweep the skeptical Dahlia off her feet during each moment leading up to his departure.

"He took me home to meet his family. He told me he would never bring anyone to meet his family unless he was serious. And I guess he thought this was serious, but I wasn't sure. But I did like the family—we had a nice time."

"He kept writing—two letters a day—more mail than I ever got in my life. I was bombarded with letters, addressed to the most wonderful girl in the world, and I thought, well, I don't know about that."

Al stayed in the Army for four years. He started in Abilene, Texas that November. He got a 15 day furlough every six months.

"I was the Provost Sergeant, you know. I had a staff car, a driver, a motorcycle with an Indian (side-car). I put all the furloughs together, so I made sure I had three days to travel there, 10 days to stay, and then two days to travel back."

Each spring, Al came home and took Dahlia to Easter Mass. He always provided her with a gardenia corsage. "I always loved the smell, so so sweet," she remembered.

After three years in Texas, Al asked to be shipped overseas. First, he was sent to Indian Gap, Pennsylvania, and then Camp Beele in California. Finally he got his wish to help 'finish the job' and went Pearl Harbor, then to the Northern Luzon in the Philippines, and finally to New Guinea.

"I was Head Postal Clerk by then," he remembered suddenly, as if that whole chapter of his life hadn't been opened in decades.

During his second year in Texas, Dahlia and Alphonse became engaged. They wanted to get married right away.

"Both families were against it because I was so young, and if something happened to him I would be left alone. When Joe said no, I told Joe to mind his own business. I never dared to say such a thing to my brother before. I said, 'you're married, why can't I?'"

Her father, Giovanni, was not even consulted.

"I had intentions of going to Texas. He had an apartment and I had my trousseau and my pretty light green suit and a cape that Alice and Sue bought. My sisters were happy. I was ready to go to Texas and get married but that didn't pan out. He was getting shipped out and couldn't leave me alone down there."

Al returned home to Providence in February of 1946 after his tour in New Guinea and the Philippines. Three months later, on May 6, my parents were married at Holy Ghost Church, just like Maria and Giovanni, and like Philomena and Emilio. The Testas threw the reception at their home on Dover Street. More than 200 people flowed in and out of the house, through the yard celebrating. Al's mother Jenny served a hot and cold buffet, which she made along with her sister-in-law Margaret—Uncle Rocco DeLuca's wife. And Jenny made the wedding cake: three tiers of almond flavored white cake with white butter cream frosting, decorated with little edible silver balls.

Jenny knew how to entertain, and the Testas loved throwing big parties with lots of food and wine and laughter. When the house was full it was a happy festive place to be.

My parents traveled together to New York City on their honeymoon, and stayed at the Hotel Taft. They hit all the hot spots: the Copa Cabana, Zanzibar to hear the Mills Brothers, and the Latin Quarters to hear Xavier Cougart.

"All the boys were coming home and we couldn't find a place to live, so we stayed with his parents." Dahlia went to work at Gladding's department store and Alphonse went to work at the Central Market. By December of that same year, my mother became pregnant. Marie Arlene Testa was born in September of 1947. "She was beautiful—with blond hair and blue eyes like her dad."

Life continued to move quickly. Perhaps too quickly

My father wiped the apple turnover crumbs off his face. The color returned to his face now. Maybe it was a sugar high, but maybe not. My mother sat back on her perch with a smile on her face. I didn't pry; I just relaxed and watched them. I could tell they were back there together, at Club Zanzibar, eating almond-flavored wedding cake, and looking at their beautiful baby girl.

NOVEMBER 1942

Dahlia in front of Uncas Manufacturing

DOVER STREET

Alphonse and Dahlia began life together on 153 Dover Street, along with his parents Anthony (Tony) Testa and Giovannina (Jenny) DeLuca Testa.

The small, tidy bungalow in the Mount Pleasant section of Providence, with voluptuous, pale blue hydrangea bushes in front and perpetual vegetable gardens in back, reflected style, order, and many, many ominous feelings. I could feel them whenever I visited, like they were happy to see us but underneath all the smiles lay sadness, darkness, hopelessness. No matter how many times I blessed myself with the numerous holy water receptacles throughout the house, or how hard I stared at the crosses woven from blessed palms, the sadness could not be erased.

The house looked no different in the 60s and 70s than in 1946, when my mother moved in. The first floor housed three small, dark bedrooms, each with mahogany furnishings and a pale crucifix on the wall that almost glowed (as I child I thought they were glow-in-the-dark but was promptly corrected). The eat-in kitchen had a pale green Formica table and chair set, a pantry where my grandmother both prepared meals and also performed rituals over water and oil to ward off the malocchia in order to soothe someone's headache, or determine whether a particular visitor meant harm or good.

The dining room held more mahogany—a beautiful Chippendale set for Sunday dinner and holidays, then a pale living room and the one bright spot—my grandmother's sun parlor, bursting with African violets, ferns, lilies and other silent, peaceful life forms. There was a big white wooden chair with a blanket customized with the name Testa in red. I thought this was the most special chair in the world, though I was never allowed to sit on it.

Upstairs in the attic the summer air stagnated, the winter air froze your breath, and the times in between allowed us kids a perfect escape from the pressure of family interactions. My Grandfather Tony's escape was downstairs in the cellar, where he tinkered with tools, hoarded old newspapers and avoided the rest of his family. Both areas seemed pretty much off limits to my mother when she moved in. My parents, my grandparents, and their three remaining daughters all lived on that first floor until my sister Maree was born in 1947.

My mother's metamorphosis from indulged little Dahlia, with a full assemblage of parents and brothers and sisters to shield her from pain, distract her with laughter and provide an audience for her animal sounds and tap dancing serenades, into Mrs. Testa began on Dover Street. Her own mother could no longer comfort her, or snuggle her at night while her father worked the night shift. That same mother who, sickly for as long she Dahlia could remember, never complained. So as Dahlia shared her new family's home, a place where making mistakes gained more attention than making jokes, my mother assumed she held no right to complain. Her own mother never complained, no matter how sick she was. She rolled out noodles and cooked for her family with a smile. So Dahlia must not question her frustration and confusion. This mantra played over and over in her head during the next few years.

Dahlia still had her sisters, Phil, Alice, and Sue. Phil always tried to help but certainly had her own issues with a bakery to run and five very active children of her own. Sue and Alice never found anyone good enough to marry, so they lived together, worrying about their Dale, about how they could help without Al resenting the interference. Al desired neither charity nor advice. His lack of understanding and appreciation for the Fiore way of life was obvious. His own family treated each other seriously and severely. Criticisms and punishments were many and harsh, to necessitate the proper decorum. One remembrance that turned my stomach as a child was when my father, a young boy, suffered a stab with a fork at the dinner table that drew blood; Tony's disapproval, for reaching over when he shouldn't have. And although lively music did play on Dover Street, ala the Testa Family Orchestra, grudges, silences, and regrets provided a sinister undertone.

My father enjoyed the Fiores, but lacked the confidence to become part of the family. Not to mention his skin—so very light—his blonde hair, and his intense corn flower blue eyes. He looked more German than Italian—very different looking from the darker, Fiores. They were wary of him too, so proper, so serious, so pale—so easy to tease.

Living in that house on Dover Street after living on Marshall Street certainly presented my mother with some challenges. She loved her husband

and longed for acceptance from her new family. But high standards, somber moods and co-habitation stress isolated her.

My grandfather Tony owned a grocery store before the Great Depression, and then lost it all when the market crashed. From wealthy small businessman to sad angry man tinkering in the cellar, often constructing boobie traps for burglars with tin cans. Even as a wealthy man, he had lacked peace or contentment. He had his music, his violin. But his desire for order, discipline and perfection resulted in intolerance and impatience with his wife and children. Tony shared those blue eyes with my father, but Tony's cast a chill wherever they looked. He walked everywhere, never drove during my lifetime. That "he was not an easy man to live with" only scratched the surface.

I don't remember too much about Tony at all. By the time I came along in 1964 he was well into his seventies and I was just another grandchild to add to the list. We never had a conversation. I just went up to him and gave him a kiss hello, and then a kiss goodbye—if he wasn't in the cellar that is. He treated me kindly, if not personally, always providing cigar-scented hugs and, on holidays or special occasions, stuffing an envelope with a few dollars into my hands. These small cash gifts always came separate and apart from anything my grandmother gave me. Always in a white envelope that said "Love, Grandpa" and nothing else. When I graduated from high school he gave me $5 with an actual card. These gifts were small but they were his money. I also remember that he ate butterscotch candy constantly and was never sick a day in his life until he hit his 90s and even then he wasn't so much physically ill as he began to develop an overall sense of dementia. Once as the family sat around sorting through old photo albums, he picked up a black and white picture of me in a sailor dress when I was about four years old and looked at it, puzzled. "Who do you think that is, Pop?" Auntie Dot said. And, he said, "I'm not sure, but she looks like she could be one of us."

After Tony hit 100, my Auntie Dot, another of my aunts who never married, decided, along with my father, that it was time to put Tony in the VA home. Either he couldn't or he didn't want to, control his bodily functions, and Auntie Dot, who was in her 70s by this time, could no longer take care of herself and him. Plus, it wasn't until he was this far gone that he couldn't put up a fight about going. Even at 99 years old, Tony held the authority over his elderly children. They respected him until the end and feared him for almost as long.

I went to see him a few times at the VA, but he really had no clue who I was or why I was there. I usually went with my sister Donna and my mother. He remembered my mother, always kindly. Then, after 103 years of butterscotch and cigars, Tony passed on.

My grandmother Jenny, a phenomenal baker, cook, homemaker, and president of the Rhode Island PTA, shared a house with Tony but little else. Something came between them, something unknown to me, something no one understands enough or can admit to enough to share. Whatever it was, it caused her to rip her wedding picture in half. I actually have a copy of the picture scotch taped back together. They look perfectly costumed, and too serious to be happy. Their marital problems may have had something to do with my Grandfather losing everything during the Depression. They had to put the house in my Grandmother's name so that no one could take it from them. I doubt this concession went over easy with him. Removing him from the deed, from owning anything or earning anything, put him at a disadvantage that was likely too difficult for him to bear. So began his withdrawal from society and his beginning as the cellar hermit. The most he did in the world outside was walk around downtown Providence, often from sunrise to sunset.

Jenny Testa differed from Maria Fiore. She was loud, opinionated, and did what she felt needed to be done exactly when she wanted. Just because her husband decided to give up and go underground was no reason for her to follow. She took trips to Pennsylvania Dutch Country and Niagara Falls with my Auntie Dot and other lady friends. She shopped, she entertained. And she suffered from more ailments than I can list here—some very real and some not so much. She craved attention, and needed to see everyone lively and gregarious and happy with her in the center, getting the praise, the respect, the adoration. Perhaps it compensated for what she didn't get from Tony.

Dover Street served as the setting for my mother's beginning as a wife, mother and daughter-in-law. Neither of my parents experienced sufficient preparation for adult life. My father's time in the Army served as more of a vacation from the regimentation of Dover Street, although he won't admit that now. And I don't want him to.

All parents, most parents, do what they think is best for their children, even if it's masked by a barrage of personality disorders, insecurities and unfulfilled dreams. That's what I believe, and I hope that's what my father believes about his family. The Testas loved my mother, but were highly critical, and placed enormous, unachievable expectations upon her. Such pressure never existed in her life before, and she did not take well to it.

My father, always intelligent and studious, handled the too great expectations differently. He got offered the opportunity to go to law school by his Uncle Carl, Tony's brother. Carl, a lawyer himself, served as a judge in Providence and lived a proud, decorated life. I don't know what made my father turn him down. We'll get to that, I'm sure, as we discuss the old times. But the last thing I want is for my father to feel sad or unfulfilled at 91. My parents, like their parents, did the best they knew how.

On Dover Street for my Aunt Elaine's wedding.
L to R—Dahlia, Alphonse holding Maree, Jenny and Tony.

IRON BALLS

Once my sister Maree came along in 1947, my parents realized they must find a place of their own. They journeyed a few streets away from the Testas on Dover Street, and since they didn't own a car, the Mount Pleasant section of Providence provided the convenience of being close to Dover Street, as well as to my father's work at the A&P, and to almost all of the Fiore and Testa relatives. One giant step for Al and Dale, one tiny leap towards real independence.

Mrs. P, my parents' first official landlady in their first official apartment on 49 Andem Street, started out nice enough. "All of them started out nice," my mother told me. "But it wouldn't be long before it would start. Sometimes little by little. Sometimes all at once. But they were all crazy."

On the plus side, Andem Street held the luxury of six whole rooms to spread out in. No more stuffing everything they owned into one bedroom, or having various Testas watching every gesture and movement. No more sharing a bathroom with four other women.

My parents could afford the $35 a month rent, for that pretty much was the sum total of my father's monthly pay. They didn't need a phone, or new clothes, and the baby did fine with hand-me-downs from the relatives. Andem Street came 'furnished' with a rocking chair in the den, and a living room sofa. Add a crib, bed, stove and icebox, and you've got paradise.

One tiny caveat of the dwelling was Mrs. P's back door rule, which prohibited the newlyweds and their five month old Maree from either entering or exiting via the front door. A small concession they could manage, strange as it seemed.

Notwithstanding the sparse furnishings, and the back door rule, Andem Street truly did start out as paradise. They didn't eat at home much, which was a good thing since my mother could only afford to buy a half pound of hamburger a week. Once again, family came through with the necessary victuals to keep the trio going.

My mother was pretty sure Mrs. P hit Mr. P on a regular basis. Vicious, I believe, is the word my mother used to describe her.

She petrified my mother, and appeared to enjoy doing so. Apparently Mrs. P didn't act this way towards my father, so perhaps a sort of Gas Lighting phenomenon was intended towards my mother. That's how it felt to her, anyway.

Also known by my mother as The Interrogator, because everyone must have a nickname in Fioreland, Mrs. P demanded my parents bring Maree's carriage up three flights of stairs each day to their third floor apartment. She did not want a baby carriage in the back doorway or, God forbid, against the house near the back door.

Each day after my father walked off to work in the city, my mother carefully placed a fully dressed Maree in her crib and, keeping the door open so she could hear her, carried the clunky carriage downstairs three flights to the back doorway. By the way, 1947 parents had no notion of the convenient collapsible strollers we use today, or of the miracle of the handy umbrella stroller either. Moms and Dads of the 1940's lugged around full-blown prams, with white spoke wheels and room for a small nursery school inside. The chassis did collapse a bit, if that's what you want to call it, but those chrome-plated steel contraptions cannot compare to the compact plastic ones we use today.

After bringing down the carriage, my mother would then race up three flights and get to Maree as quickly as she could, fearing that something dreadful would happen to her baby girl through each eternity of maneuvering the unwieldy creature of a pram around three narrow staircases. Once at the summit, she'd carry Maree down three flights as fast as she could so as not to leave the carriage unattended too long. With that little ritual completed, Dahlia and her baby girl were free for the day.

Each day my mother "visited" with different relatives. One day it would be her sister Phil, another, her mother-in-law on Dover Street, and yet another with brother Joe and his wife Gilda. Come to find out, Mrs. P didn't really like noise, or people for that matter, and my mother feared losing her luxurious six-room wonderland due to breathing too loudly. At the end of each work day, my father picked my mother up from her visit on his walk home, and the three of them strolled back to paradise.

Then, while my father maneuvered the carriage back upstairs, Mrs. P would catch my mother with the baby in her arms at the door.

"Did you have company last night?" She'd ask innocently. "There was so much noise upstairs I thought you were having a party! And the baby, was she playing with an iron ball? All I heard was her banging an iron ball on the floor all night."

At five-months old, Maree could not walk, and was not prone to playing with iron balls, even if my mother was insane enough to provide her with them. My mother took Mrs. P's criticisms literally. She couldn't understand how anyone would think a civilized parent would give a baby iron balls to play with. Unfortunately for my mother, it was Mrs. P who had the iron balls. By Maree's first birthday, my parents moved out of paradise and into something entirely different.

From Mrs. P, the Testa trio moved in with my Aunt Phil and Uncle Emilio—actually right upstairs from them on the third floor of Murphy Street where they lived on the second floor and ran a bakery on the first. And while my mother adored her sister Phil and her brother-in-law Emilio, and all her little nieces and nephews, the two families together under one roof strained the sisters' relationship. Phil, neither the tidiest nor most disciplined of the sisters, had little interest in housework or scolding her children. Phil had plenty of money from the bakery she owned with Emilio, and she used the money to have someone else come and clean, a black lady, my mother said. "The poor thing would scrub that house, and the minute she left they'd turn it upside down again." Phil had difficulty understanding why Al made so little money and why he couldn't give Dale more to spend on groceries, or on herself for that matter. Hearing this shamed my mother, and she bridled up in defensiveness. "I told her it was none of her business," my mother said, "and I immediately felt horrible about snapping." Dale felt obligated to defend her husband. "Things weren't the same for a long time after that," she remembered. The Testa trio lived on Murphy Street for 12 months and then moved yet again.

They next found another house in Providence, on Mount Pleasant Avenue. My brother Al, Alphonse Robert Testa Jr., came along during this time. Why someone would want to make a junior out of that name haunts me to this day. My brother became Alley, or Young Al to the family.

My parents enjoyed living on Mount Pleasant Avenue. There still wasn't much furniture, but they had a living room rug to sit on. They lived across the street from Mount Pleasant High school, and Maree attended the elementary school around the corner. Mom walked Maree back and forth to school with Al in the stroller, when he would stay in the stroller, that is. A hard one to manage that Al was. Not a quiet child, he did make quite a fuss, and quite often at that, putting my mother through the proverbial wringer. My mother did all she could to manage him, but he was tough compared to Maree. The things he would do as a toddler, like lock my mother out of the house and proceed to then lean against the screen on the third floor open window—caused her more than her share of angst.

The V's owned the house on Mount Pleasant Avenue, and seemed fine until Mr. V could no longer stand Al's crying and fussing. Suddenly, the V's son was getting married and they needed the tenement for him and his bride, or so they said. My mother believes it was an excuse to get rid of them.

Staying in the Mount Pleasant area of Providence, my family next moved to a house on the corner of Beaufort and Carleton Streets, where they remained for the next three years. There lived another crazy one, according to my mother. This landlady took to screaming and yelling a lot, mostly at my mother, and usually calling her names like slob and pig while my mother went through her third pregnancy with my sister Jane. I'm sure Dahlia felt like a bit of a slob with no outdoor clothesline and no washing machine. The family of four lived in an apartment filled with clotheslines, with sheets hanging for the kids to continually run through and knock to the ground. All the laundry was done by my mother in the bathtub, including the dirty diapers.

Two of my siblings were born with some level of defect to their left eyes, a slight turn that required costly surgery. All of these factors over time, coupled with my mother's determination not to complain, or let on to her family that she felt as if she were failing miserably, caused her great emotional sickness.

Dahlia began to tire emotionally and physically. Exhaustion and crazy landladies and crooked-eyed kids eroded my mother's normally laid-back disposition. Once she lived a child's carefree life, when there was always someone there to take care of her. And then her mother Maria left her. Before she had time to get over her loss, she married my father and became part of a new family that was just so different from the Fiores. She felt unprepared and under-qualified for her new responsibilities. Because of all this, she took criticism deeply and personally.

It wasn't long before her body and mind began to strain and tire and long for peace, without hushing children and scrubbing baby shit out of a seemingly never-ending conveyor belt of dirty diapers.

Dahlia and friend at Sand Hill Cove Beach in Narragansett, RI.

EVIL EYES

This story marks the beginning of an intensely upsetting part of my mother's life. I thank her for sharing this with me as her daughter, and with you as our readers. My mother's journey was always a little hazy to me. I only found out about her 1955 nervous breakdown about 10 or 15 years ago, the last of her children to know about my mother's shameful secret. I think writing about life and talking together have helped her realize there is no shame in being ill, especially after making such a brave recovery. It's helped me understand the strands of depression and anxiety that are woven throughout my family's story—and my own story too.

"When you don't want to do something, it works on your mind," my mother says to me now. My mother did a lot of things because others wanted her to. She became what most psychologists would call a "People Pleaser," at least that's what my counselor calls me. People with strong personalities and narcissistic tendencies feed off People Pleasers like leeches feed off a blood bank.

If I hadn't already invested the hours and the dollars into psychotherapy myself, I would not even attempt to play Doctor Freud here. But my assessment is that this act of avoiding conflict rooted itself in her older siblings taking care of Dahlia when her own mother was sick. Her brothers told her how to act. Her sister Phil scooped her off to her house each time Maria was too ill to care for her. And Dahlia went along, letting them all make the decisions and did what she was told—always. In an environment of constant illness paired with Italian culture, Dahlia fulfilled the expectations for most young girls: listen to her father and her big brothers and then, in time, listen to her husband. She gave the reins to her family and trusted them without question.

Being a delicate flower is fine as a girl. But as an adult woman, it's impossible. So somewhere in this transition she went from being directed on the straight and narrow to feeling forced to do things against her will. The results were devastating, but unavoidable.

The Z's, a kindly Portuguese couple from Fall River Massachusetts, owned a big beautiful beach house in Narragansett. As my mother felt weaker, had more trouble sleeping and more difficulty keeping food down, the Testas and the Z's decided that a week at the beach would help her. My mother was not interested, but felt she had no choice but to go.

She didn't sleep for a week. A heavy cloud held over Dahlia, an uneasiness and eeriness that are hard to describe. *Was she there alone?* She couldn't tell.

My Grandma Jenny insisted my mother invite the Z's to dinner a few months before this, and ask them to be my sister Jane's godparents. My father offered my mother no help, as he would never go against his own mother's request. I wonder if he even knew my mother protested. She kept so much in. His frustration was probably just as severe as hers.

Mr. and Mrs. Z bought the baby all sorts of luxurious and beautiful gifts that offered no usefulness—satin shoes and blankets that you dare not soil. After my mother got sick, after a week at their splendid beach house, my family never saw the Z's again. To this day, my sister has never met her godparents.

Mr. and Mrs. Z specialized in the creation and distribution of potions to ward off the Malocchia—better known as The Evil Eye. Their 'Gift' was well-known to the women—and men—who traveled in my Grandma Jenny's social circle in the Mount Pleasant area of Providence during the late 1940s and early 50s.

If pressed, nearly anyone who is Italian, Portuguese, or Spanish—actually, ask almost anyone over 30 years old of Indo-European ancestry and he or she may inform you of his or her family's own version of the Evil Eye. While younger people may refer to such superstitions with humor, older folks only share with reluctant caution. Regardless of cultural origin, this evil power is thought to cause all kinds of maladies, from headaches to disease to infertility. The mere mention of the Evil Eye can cause harm to those who are standing near to the speaker. Like Harry Potter's Lord Voldemort, it's *the Thing that can't be Mentioned.*

According to Italian Folklore, the person giving the Malocchia isn't necessarily evil, but if he or she envies something of yours, your home, your children, anything, and thinks for just a split second—why her—why not me?—a mere snippet of envy—intended or not—can birth disaster.

Remedies used to ward off the Malocchia vary based on village and individual family secret tradition. One common Italian method is to wave one's hand in the direction of the unknowing evil-doer while making what looks strangely like symbol for *I Love You* in Sign Language. The only difference is that your thumb holds down your bent index and middle fingers instead of sticking straight out, and you kind of point the pinkie and index fingers outward, like your hand is a little bull with horns pointing towards the offender.

The real Italian word for the Evil Eye is *mano cornuto*—or horned hand. To me, it appears rather obnoxious to be waving a bull hand in someone's face as he or she is complimenting you. Nevertheless, growing up in a predominantly Italian town, my schoolmates and I often threw this gesture, thinking we were giving the Malocchia instead of warding it off. Silly children, getting our voodoo all mixed up! I, of course, convinced myself at an early age that I held this power to curse. Even into my early adulthood, I jokingly pointed the little bull at a friend when he wasn't looking while a group of us walked along the beach. Just a joke meant to amuse my other friends. A moment after my shamanism, he was stung by a jelly fish—proof of my awesome powers.

On Dover Street, the Malocchia generally caused very bad headaches, always brought into the house by visitors, known and unknown. Many times Jenny slipped away to perform her incantations, even while company unknowingly visited in her parlor. If she emerged with a look of disdain, it was not going to be a pleasant evening. Or if one of my aunts complained of a headache, Jenny scooted into the pantry, to her ceramic bowl near the sink filled with water. She'd splash the olive oil in while reciting secret prayers handed down through generations of DeLuca family women. Depending on where the bubbles landed, you may lose the headache, or you may not.

The Fiores never practiced Malocchia, as they considered it black magic and evil. My mother could hardly believe her own dear mother-in-law to be nothing short of a sorceress. There was the bowl, sitting beside the pantry sink, filled with water and an oozy coating of leftover olive oil, waiting for its next assignment. Many times Jenny slid into the pantry only to find her water bowl empty, scrubbed clean of its slippery oil and drying on the dish rack. Who would dare do such a thing? Her family needed protection and whoever couldn't understand that was surely not right in the head. Sometimes my mother would fess up, but only to say she was doing the dishes and thought her magic bowl one more dirty dish in need of a wash.

Between the oil and water ritual and the horseshoe over the back doorway, another folk remedy to keep luck inside the house while deflecting outside evil, the Testas appeared pretty adequately covered. But Grandma Jenny apparently wasn't easily convinced. Her mission to keep the Malocchia away from her family, to ensure their prosperity in the face of all that envy out there could not be taken for granted. Perhaps she blamed Malocchia for my grandfather's loss of his grocery store, and shortly thereafter his lack of interest in her and everyone around him. Maybe someone envied what she had—a good man with a good living, money, and proper children. Protecting her children became her mission. They were all she had left—the only people in that house on Dover Street that still paid her any mind.

That's where the Z's came in.

My mother believed in the Z's even less than she did in the Malocchia—although she did consider them to be very kind, generous people.

Pulling up to the Z's magnificent home in Fall River, Massachusetts with the whole Testa family became a monthly ritual. Sundays after church, the family would head out, my parents, my grandmother, Maree and Al. Maree still remembers the bumpy rides in the car over the old Braga Bridge, and this retreat of a home, complete with its own chapel and a life-sized, full color statue of Jesus at its door.

The Z's gave, if that's what you want to call it, my family all kinds of charms meant to keep the Evil Eye away. Strange little bottles filled with liquid—oil, water, and other unknown things that combined together could ward off danger, help you sleep at night, make you right. While Grandma Jenny ate this up, my mother felt like throwing up every time she was given some little something to keep in her purse or her dresser drawer. She dumped many such gifts in the woods or buried them at the bottom of the trash so no one would see, wondering if such rejection could also cause a curse to fall upon her or her family. After much inner battling, her fear of dark magic won out over her obligation to mind her elders. Choosing to secretly destroy this evil wore on my mother, for she told no one. Not her sisters, not her husband.

"No one has the power to do that to you," she tells me now.

I wouldn't have listened to my mother had she told me before. Before, when I spent so many years as a People Pleaser. I thought love equaled putting yourself last, putting up with pain and revulsion and even the loss of your dignity. People Pleasers consider anything to the contrary as absolute rebellion, and rebellion and love do not mix. That's the way I saw it. I have changed, thankfully, and the change has not been easy or natural. I sometimes wish I had known about my mother sooner, about not letting others control you, a lot sooner. But my battle has made me stronger, and made me a better fighter when I need to protect myself and the people I love. Plus, I know I would not have listened. You had to be there.

"Better to bear the shame than the pain" was a saying that my Grandma Jenny associated with flatulence. My mother took that message to heart beyond body functions. Only to her, in those early years of her marriage, she thought she could bear pain and conflict. Suffocate it and, therefore, destroy it. But all that negative energy cannot be stifled. It finds its way out, no matter how much you try to deny it. It will not be denied. Just like a fart.

I understand the knot that must have throbbed in my mother's gut. Her sweaty neck and wringing hands that she hoped no one would notice. I wish I had been there back then to help her, to tell her what I learned the hard way about standing up for yourself. I wish I hadn't shut my mother out of my life when I needed her guidance the most. We both traveled down similar paths of conflict, anxiety and fear, of shame and isolation. And I thought we were so different.

My daughter Julia just turned 12 and is already beginning to pull away from me. Not intentionally, it's just part of the dance from little girl, to adolescent, to young woman. Everything I say is met with rolled eyes and raised eyebrows. All the other mothers are cooler than me. If given the choice between an electronic tablet and a conversation with me, the tablet will win hands down.

I am trying to brace myself for this ride. I am determined not to let the door shut all the way. I never want her to experience the torment my mother and I did with no one to turn to. When I ask my mother about this, she tells me to wait and be patient. "She'll come back. They always come back," she says. I know she's right, but I don't want anyone or anything to hurt her while I'm waiting.

Four Generations—L to R—my sister Maree holding her daughter Dawne, Grandma Jenny, and Dahlia pose at Jenny and Tony's 50th Anniversary party in 1969.

THE OLD CROW

The dizzy spells started a week before Easter—with trouble standing up and staying vertical for any extended period of time. The Old Crow rarely calls me at work because she doesn't want to bother me. I offer to drive her to Miriam Hospital and, to my surprise, she immediately agrees.

Some of the dizziness is mostly likely due to new blood pressure meds. She dehydrates easily now; her potassium levels get too low. But she's still a tough old bird—her heart remains strong; she still manages to scratch at her lawn with the rake, pull up weeds from her garden, or venture out in the winter to clear the occasional dusting of snow from the walkway before we can stop her.

My mother rarely feels unwell for an extended period of time. Normally she avoids hospitals, doctors and medicine, and usually denies symptoms until the last minute. But now that she's well into her 80's, she wants answers when she suffers an ailment. She needs closure. What is making her dizzy?

At 91 years old, the idea of my father driving her anywhere—never mind through the winding hills of Providence—brings on immediate queasiness. The dread I feel, that all of my siblings probably feel escalates, as we envision my father stubbornly crawling his Buick up and around the tight streets of the East Side, clinging to the sidewalk, knocking over pedestrians who dare to venture out. I must take her.

The Old Crow will tell you that yard work and caffeine preserved her sanity through the years. When we were young she would down three or four pots of coffee a day and go like a madwoman—making beds, doing dishes, cleaning toilets and picking up all the garbage we'd leave laying around on the floor, the kitchen table, her beautiful Chippendale mahogany dining room set. Damp towels left on the floor after a shower. She would pick up like a hired servant while we all obliged her by living like hotel guests. As my father usually found fault with the way any of us girls did chores—and heaven forbid my brother did anything—my mother did it all herself, mostly to avoid an unnecessary argument. Of course we never learned how to do anything really domestic, so that housekeeping then thrust itself upon us as adults without warning. Karma works like that, as each of us became indentured servants to our respective families.

We girls did get to cook with her though, and bake. I loved rolling out dough, wearing an oversized apron or a *moppine* around me, while I dusted flour all over my wooden rolling pin and the linoleum floor. My mother convinced me that the incredibly old rolling pin without handles had been sized especially for me. I believed her, admiring myself in the reflection of the toaster, often using the hollow roller as a telescope. I remember making cinnamon pinwheels—the gritty sweetness of sprinkled sugar and cinnamon together on the dough—adding dabs of butter, rolling, and slicing with a blunt butter knife. Holding them together carefully, placing each one gently on a cookie tray, counting the minutes before they finished baking and could be devoured with ice cold milk.

I remember making lasagna—plopping spoonfuls of ricotta cheese onto steaming crisscross sheets of lasagna noodles. I got to dunk the ladle into the pot and my mother held onto it with me so that the thick, cold tomato gravy spread evenly over each layer of pasta. While sprinkling chunks of cubed mozzarella and pepperoni, I usually managed to sneak a few samples, hiding them in my chubby fist like a magician doing the quarter trick. My sister Donna and I still remember my mother's 'lasagna sweater,' a fuzzy white sweater with a plaid cowl neck. When we saw that sweater, we knew lasagna would be in the oven bubbling away in short order.

Even when I wasn't helping, it was pleasure enough just to be with her in the kitchen, lying on the naugahide bench, sliding myself in under the kitchen table, listening to and feeling the buzz of a hand mixer or the blender. I still enjoy white noise and the tremble of household tools. As she vacuumed on Saturday mornings, I'd lounge on the couch with my eyes closed and let my mind go blank, feeling the goose bumps up and down my arms and legs. Even now when I happen to catch the cleaning crew at work pushing their industrial-sized vacuums towards my office, I find myself hanging around to listen. Unfortunately the white noise doesn't have the same effect on me when I'm doing the vacuuming.

Now she's off to get a CAT scan, as I pass the time watching people and checking my cell phone, which isn't supposed to be on. A few years ago I would panic every time my parents had to go to the hospital, thinking that it was—*it*. My lungs, my heart, and my stomach all melted and sizzled like butter into eggs on blazing asphalt. Swallowing back the stench of my fried innards, I held my tongue, gazed blankly and uttered monotones for their sake. Now I'm used to this, used to the little episodes that accompany old age and need immediate attention, used to the patient coming home with me that day or maybe just staying overnight for observation. Now that I'm used to all this my mind doesn't race as much when I wait. I pass the time listing off the possibilities based on past experiences. Perhaps a UTI (urinary tract infection), that can sometimes be insidious and deadly for the elderly. Such an infection can travel throughout the body—even to the brain—without symptoms. Or maybe just vertigo, from self-induced stress or just from being 87 going on 88.

I always sensed a panic in my mother at the mere mention of her going to the doctors, never mind the hospital. Growing up I assumed that's how all mothers felt. I noticed nothing extreme, but nevertheless I sensed something different about my mother—not bad, just different. I knew my mother worried a lot about a lot of things. She didn't drive a car, didn't have a lot of friends to go shopping with, or to hang around drinking coffee with. She couldn't swim, but loved the ocean. Standing there knee deep and holding my hand while the waves slapped us gently. Lots of things frightened her: thunder storms, or kids climbing too high, running too fast. I was the last kid to get to ride my bike in the street, the last one to walk to Heyward's penny candy store, the last one to do a lot of things that most kids in the neighborhood got to do without parental anguish.

It happened nine years before I was born, in 1955. Not suddenly, of course, but building up bit by bit, up to a very sharp, dangerous point.

All of the moving from tenement to tenement, the washing diapers for three in the bathtub, no time for laughter, or doing animal interpretations and tap dances for company. All of the chores that she couldn't do right, couldn't do well enough. Everyone telling her what to do. The tall lean grey cat she married that used to address letters to the most wonderful girl in the world changed. My father grew frustrated with her indecision. She let him call all the shots, make all the decisions. And when he didn't, his mother did. And she let them. That's what she thought a good wife, a delicate flower, was supposed to do.

As a girl she let her brothers and sisters protect her. But this was more, not just protection, but dismissal because Dahlia feared making decisions. She wasn't used to it and didn't think she knew how. My mother was not used to conflict, either. She feared it and avoided it at all costs. Too much noise meant they might have to move again. The price—keep it inside and allow it to fester.

And while Dahlia adored her children, she spent all her time with them, every single moment of every single day. And although she appreciated the Z's kindness, she didn't want them to be Jane's godparents. She didn't believe in their potions and amulets. She was full of fear—fear that her husband wouldn't think she was good enough, fear that her siblings didn't think he was good enough, fear of her mother-in-law, of the malocchia, fear of the incantations and the amulets, that someone would find them buried in the ground, fear that the family would have to drag its paltry belongings to yet another tenement with yet another crazy landlady, fear that they couldn't pay the rent. Fear of anyone seeing how frightened she was.

By the time it all happened, Dahlia had stopped eating and was down to 98 pounds, at least thirty pounds off regular weight. Summertime, the hot dry air whipped along the Narragansett coastline. Her body sat in her beach chair, on the blistering sand. But her mind was some place different. Dahlia saw the sand and the sky and the water blurring together and bubbling over and over her. In desperation, she struggled to rise but it was no use. She tried to reach up, to kick and claw her way out, but there was a glass lid that she couldn't break—no matter how hard she slammed her clenched fists. Dahlia was drowning in the sand. Her brothers Danny and Reynolds sat by and watched her with concern. She didn't recognize them. They took her to Chapin Hospital in Providence. She was admitted with severe depression.

Electroconvulsive therapy (ECT), formerly known as electroshock therapy was used to draw patients out of very deep depression. The most devastating side effect, aside from the pain, was memory loss. For three weeks she endured this torture, trading her memories in order to crack through the top of that glass lid.

"Look at the pig!" the hospital attendant heckled while she shivered uncontrollably in a tub full of ice. Naked, and bleeding with her period, she despised this man who didn't know her, didn't know how beautiful she looked in her wedding dress, in the suits that Sue and Alice bought for her, in any outfit, any clothes at all. "I just kept praying to Jesus the whole time. I kept seeing God and that's what got me through it," she told me. "They treated me worse than an animal. I wouldn't treat an animal they way they treated me."

Taking her clothes, forcing her and the other women patients to be observed naked, while male attendants glared and smiled—evil smirks meant to humiliate. Scared women cowering in fear and disgust. Was this some tried and true method of rehabilitation for the emotionally ill? She never felt safe, never felt in control.

As she described this horror to me, all I kept envisioning was a black and white movie, *Harvey,* maybe. Always a favorite up to this point—many times I have risen extra early on Easter Sundays to watch before my husband and daughter awaken. Except now it isn't so funny. Now envisioning Elwood P Dowd's sister Veta getting stripped of her clothes against her will and thrown into a cold bath at the sanitarium, I'm embarrassed for her, enraged at them. No longer funny when it's your mother suffering.

Her memories coincide well with the state of mental health care in the US during the 1950s. Funds for mental health research were sorely lacking at this time, while funds flowed freely towards other types of medical research—cancer, for example. Areas that perhaps didn't hold the social stigma of mental illness. But the numbers of those suffering from depression, anxiety and other issues continued to rise, while the number of trained professionals available to help them did not, causing the state of mental institutions to diminish into little more than chaotic holding centers, less focused on care than crowd control. The patients suffered greatly, with few advocates and too many unqualified dregs in need of work taking care of those fragile souls in need of understanding and compassion. Instead they got catcalls and filthy leering looks. Probably a lot more than looks.

She survived three weeks. Three weeks without seeing her family. Three weeks of inhumanity. All she could see was God. Strapped down in her bed, strapped down with a rubber bit in her mouth like a mare gone mad. She didn't see anyone but God.

She didn't want to see her husband. "You don't want to see the one you love the most when you're like that," she tells me now. "I probably wouldn't have recognized him anyway."

My father isn't eager to talk of it now. "I took the kids to my mother," he said quickly when I asked him what he did. "Grandma took care of the kids." I realized Jenny took care of all four of them.

After a three week eternity they let her come home, complete with enough barbiturates to take down a small herd of cattle. My mother hated that medicine, hated the way it made her feel, or rather not feel, anything. She refused to live the rest of her life in a drug-induced stupor in order to cope with the burdens married life presented. She flushed the pills down the toilet, and looked around outside for anyone lurking about with a white coat for months afterward. This may sound unreal, like a B movie. But it's true.

"Jane was nine months old and she didn't know me," my mother said. My sister, the middle child, didn't receive the same bonding experience with my mother that the rest of us did. Not to mention the fact that she fell off the bassinette when she was nine-months old. The kids were playing ball outside and the ball came in the window. When my mother turned in surprise at the shattering glass, her baby fell off the bassinette. Another in a series of incidents that broke down my mother's nerves, synapse by synapse. How would she explain this—dropping her baby—to her family, her husband, anyone?

Recovery and reintegration into daily life took a long time. The treatments and the drugs had taken almost everything in trade for her sanity. She had to teach herself all over how to do pretty much everything when she finally came home from the hospital—cook, clean, take care of children, live with her husband. Alone she re-learned the secrets of tomato gravy, creating and inhaling the slightly tangy aroma of plum tomatoes, garlic, and meatballs rolled from beef, veal and pork all together. Tomato gravy was our main staple. We enjoyed it every Sunday afternoon with macaroni and bitter escarole salad, along with garden tomatoes drizzled with olive oil and wine vinegar. During the week we made meatball sandwiches, or just plain gravy sandwiches, sometimes with firm Italian bread, sometimes with limp, spongy Wonder white. Making good satisfying tomato gravy takes hours, attention, and a sound understanding of each step—roasting the garlic and oil, running the tomatoes through a mill to get the seeds and extra pulp out, adding the tomatoes with the right ratio of water and tomato paste at the right time intervals, and making sure it simmered evenly without burning for an entire Saturday afternoon.

Or how to make what would become her own signature Christmas cookies: How to roll, chill, roll again, and cut her Twist cookies with that special little cutting wheel that I used to roll over the Formica countertop. How to make the beds, do the laundry, wash the dishes, take care of her baby girl, my sister Jane, along with her other two children, without losing her control again.

She re-learned all of the lessons Maria and Phil and Jenny taught her. She didn't want to ask for help because she didn't want them to know. She didn't want to be sent back.

My mother credits a doctor named Mangiacori with saving her life and helping her recover.

"He told me to stop taking myself so seriously. To accept that I wasn't perfect, and never would be. And to stop turning inward when things bothered me, or I would lose myself again, and he was right," she said. He helped her see that she could toughen up on the outside if she stopped holding it all in on the inside. I wish I could thank him.

My mother bravely faced and conquered many of her fears, and found herself again without the medication. Nothing could be as frightening as the alternative. She believes she recovered by learning to laugh again, and by having faith in God and herself. "When you lose your sense of humor it's a sign of emotional sickness."

As the youngest of five, I have no recollection of her struggles. In many ways I inherently became just as sheltered as little Dahlia used to be. By the time I came along, almost ten years had passed. In 1956, my parents bought a house on Greenville Avenue in Johnston, a small suburb of Providence with a large Italian American population of its own. The house, a little bungalow set back on a hill, could hardly fit the five of them, never mind a family of seven. The backyard had been cleared out of woods that reached for at least a mile. The kids could run and play and lose themselves in the woods, and make all the noise they could muster with no one to complain.

Luckily my parents moved next door to a sweet couple—Annette and Michael Pocino. Michael came straight from Italy, and his thick accent flowed as rich and smooth as the strong sweet wine he made in his cellar. He raised sheep, chickens, and assorted farm animals on Greenville Avenue, and had a cat—Conegonda—to keep the mice away.

The Pocinos brought a welcome change to my parents' lives. From the crazy landladies and the fear of eviction, they gained lifelong friends. My mother took great pleasure in asking Michael and Annette to serve as my sister Donna's godparents. They helped my parents paint and paper and put the house in order. Their chicken Cuccola came to our door each morning to cackle before going off to lay her eggs for the day. The Pocinos built a house in back of their property, where they held summer parties and the kids played house.

Donna was born in 1957, and I came along in 1964. Dahlia's two blue eyed babies were born with straight eyes and didn't have to be shushed. Life was far from perfect at that point. Many times her sanity would be tested. But she would never let it get to her—all the way—ever again.

Over time, my mother's filtering system has pretty much eroded, to the point where it's not unusual for any of us in her family to grimace in fear of what she will say next. But I'll take an Old Crow who says what's on her mind over a delicate flower with a broken stem any day. My nephew Phil really pegged her when he called her the Old Crow. The name has stuck and it suits her now. She's earned it.

She made me leave the room when she was putting her Johnny on, and I had to turn my head while the nurse came in to administer her EKG. So while the doctor, the nurse (a boy I graduated from high school with), another technician, and a number of other spare medical strangers who will never see her again attended to my topless mother, I was ordered to look away. Not with words but just a look that held her dignity. That look meant she was going to be okay, that she was not a delirious old woman who was ready for the nursing home. I gladly turned my head and let the strangers do their work.

July 4, 1945—Dahlia sitting on Dover Street on her 21st birthday. Ten months later she would be married.

LIFEBOAT

I'm squatting down, cramped, in a wooden boat that's bobbing over an icy glass blue sea. The water appears still, but a sharp breeze slices into my face. Non-descript crew members stand around like movie extras doing whatever a crew does. My mother and I both wear black rubbery scuba suits—me safely squatting inside the boat, my mother half submerged under icy blue water. I can see her, and a rope or line of some kind connects us as I try to pull her in. If I can just reach her hand. But she's slipping away from me.

The pseudo crew exerts no sense of urgency. My stomach jolts, salty sweat trickles down my face and back. The cold breeze stings my neck. My mother, pale, bloated, distressed in black slippery rubber appears resigned to her fate, but as I look closely into her deep brown eyes I see her pleading panic.

Growing up I spent many nights waking twisted and sweaty from this nightmare. Like an appendage, it's been a part of me for as far back as I can remember. As a little girl, four or five, I remember crying out and my mother coming to me, lying down next to me, trying to get me back to sleep. Petrified of returning to the boat, I clung to her. She'd wearily suggest I stare at the Virgin Mother statue on the night stand and pray for sleep. "Ask her to help you," she'd say, rubbing my back, longing to be comfortable again in her own warm bed before starting tomorrow's rituals. I clung on, the statue serving only to frighten me more. Eventually, my mother would manage to pry herself free, assuring me of God's help if only I stare at the statue. Hearing her feet shuffle back to bed, I whimpered and tried my best.

Staring at the woman in the pale blue robe holding that baby boy with a little man's face didn't help one bit. "He's making faces at me," I'd accuse, trying to squirm into my mother's bed. She'd hush me, urging me back to my own bed with a robotic desperation, for my father never allowed us into their bed, and she feared waking him. Eventually I dragged myself back to Mother Mary and the little man-baby, careful not to turn my back on them, or to stare too hard into their tiny porcelain-painted eyes.

Some nights, despite the odds, I managed to get back to sleep. Usually I'd just lay with my eyes clenched shut, pressing my fists into my eye sockets to conjure pink, purple and yellow psychedelics. I would do anything to stay away from that glaze of nearly frozen water, even if it meant ruptured eyeballs.

By the time I came along, the fifth of five children, my mother already had endured more than her allotted quota of disrupted sleep. Since my father could sleep through a militia attack, it was my mother, who could be woken by the sound of sheets rustling down the hall, who received the honor of comforting the sick, the terrified, and the bed wetters.

Once her patience and ideas ran out, she left it up to God. Aside from gazing at the statue on the nightstand, my mother's other great cure for nightmares was looking at our *Light of the World* reprint on the bedroom wall. The faux oil painting, a close-up of Baby Jesus watching over us. His face in a murky brown background, his curls entwined into his halo. His hair and face resembled mine—plump rounded features, deep set eyes and golden brown loose ringlets. Ringlets that swirled into devil horns if I squinted. And I couldn't help but squint, as the shadow of my nightlight cast a haze from the netherworlds onto the oak paneling.

I lay awake terrified as these placid faces morphed into pure evil, luring me into a land of demons, only to revert back to their holiness whenever my mother looked at them. Even still I prayed for morning, not to the picture or the statue but to my God, the nice one who understood and had nothing to do with letting little girls lie in cold sweat afraid to sleep. He'd help me.

As I fought sleep and returning to that wooden boat, thoughts rolled around in my head like kaleidoscope crystals. Why don't the good dreams come back? I'll just keep thinking about David Cassidy and I'll feel better … maybe dream about the Partridge Family … I have to save her … I don't want to go back ….

In hindsight, what were those damn crew member extras doing in my dream if they couldn't help?

Over time, the need for my mother's soothing hand on my sweaty back diminished. I replaced the statue on the nightstand with an avocado green clock-radio; Peter Frampton's wavy blonde locks replaced those of baby Jesus on my wall. I never actually told my mother about the dream; it scared me, and embarrassed me too much.

As I got older and the dream faded, my connection with my mother became looser, thinner, like a skein of yarn falling to the floor unraveling. Once the full throttle of puberty took over, my mother's opinions, requests, needs did not resonate with me. Absorbed in me, my friends, my accomplishments, my needs, my trivial conflicts. Little room existed for much more.

Now, digging down deep into myself, pushing aside the polite formality of surface feelings, I am faced with an arrogant, ugly truth. I actually had the audacity to feel superior—so much so that I didn't think I needed her. Me—college graduate, well-traveled, successful job in corporate America, married later in life after living for myself, financially independent. Her—high school drop-out, financially dependent on her husband, staying home to raise five children, never learning to drive a car.

At those times when I did make mistakes—and I did—I shut her out. How could she understand me? With 40 years between us, how could she possibly put herself in my shoes no matter how hard she tried? And I wasn't convinced she was trying hard enough anyway. Her laid-back demeanor lacked the raw sense of urgency and immediacy that drove me.

So while I achieved and complained, my mother stood by in the background, not guiding me, not interfering, always accepting whatever I presented in my usual list of demands. I assumed she, like everyone else, held no remedy for my unsettled nature. But she remained there, in case I needed to look to her for comfort. Just like the statue, just like the painting.

Only great loss could change me. A significant, great loss, with all the sorrow and feelings of helplessness that accompany it, that no advanced degree or amount of money could remedy, finally managed to wake me up.

It came after months trying, of sticking cold thermometers inside myself each morning to detect prime conceptual temperature, of reading books about determining prime vaginal mucus levels, of turning lovely moments into strained lab rat exercises. I did try to discuss my disappointment with my mother.

"Wasn't ever a problem for me," was all my mother said. I took no comfort in what I translated as her pride in her fertility, but, in reality, was a mere statement of fact. She had been bearing and raising children and caring for grandchildren since 1947. But since this was not the answer I wanted, I resented, and then ignored it.

Finally, no more tricks, no more tests, no more invasion of our privacy or our privates. What we wanted most, a little blond curly-headed baby was now in the works. We thought. Ten weeks later the bleeding started, and my husband drove me to the hospital as I leaked.

An intern scanned frantically over my abdomen. Nothing. Laying on a gurney, in a sticky mess of K-Y jelly, I wept. Not quiet, dignified weeping, but a wail, a guttural, primal wail like the kind women make on the nightly news over Middle East bloodshed. My husband stood mummified. The intern looked pale. "Hug her," she pleaded, probably hoping it would shut me up. He held me, but I couldn't feel him. I was drowning. I wanted my mother.

She came with my husband and me for the surgery. They waited together in the lounge while the remnants of my lifeless womb got wiped out. I stayed awake during it, with valium and a spinal so I was numb from the waist down and stupefied from the neck up. As *Age of Aquarius* played over speakers in the operating room, I sang along with an idiot's grin while they scraped my uterus clean. As a kid I lip-synched this song using an empty paper towel roll as my microphone, my older sisters waving the flashlight on me in the dark. I took this as a sign. Things would get better.

She didn't have to say a word, and she didn't really say much as I recall. Just having her there, to pull me out of the icy water and into the boat, was all I needed.

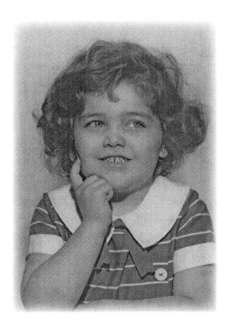

Author, circa 1967, age 3

IS THAT YOUR GRANDMOTHER?

I often wonder why daughters torture their mothers so—sometimes inadvertently, but often intentionally. Maybe not all daughters, but enough of them so that I do not feel alone in my shame for having done it, or my humiliation to for having to receive it.

My mother began having children in 1947, when she was 23 years old. She had a child every three or four years for the next decade. In 1957, when my sister Donna was born, there were four children. And four seemed to be more than enough, despite the television show that sings otherwise.

My mother got some help from time to time from her sisters, or my Grandma Jenny. They would watch the children if my mother had a dire emergency. When she was in a psychiatric hospital for three weeks in 1955, my father pretty much moved back home with this parents, taking the three children, aged eight, five and nine months, along with him. But other than that, my mother fed us, changed us, cleaned up after us, made sure we did our homework, had clothes ironed, and clean underwear ready. She cooked supper every night, with the exception of the occasional fish and chips on Fridays during Lent, when eating meat was strictly prohibited.

We did nothing to make it easy for her, hardly gave her a hand really. My Dad never changed a diaper, very rarely watched us, or took us out to give my mother a break. Or took her out to give her a break for that matter. He worked two jobs, spent many evenings out at real estate "meetings," also known as card games, and just wasn't expected to do anything domestic. We have one picture of him in the early Seventies with an apron on in front of the sink on Greenville Avenue. That's probably the only such image available and the expression on his face accurately depicts his abject horror.

Four kids, 24 hours a day, seven days a week. Then in 1964 I was born, during a thunder storm on the first day of July. Dahlia Lydia Fiore Testa, three days away from her 40th birthday, gave birth to her fifth child. Just when she thought things were starting to look up. At least that's the way I would have seen it. Donna, the youngest, was seven and a half, Maree, the oldest, seventeen. When my mother should have been breathing a sigh of relief that everyone was finally toilet trained, and when she should have been focusing on making sure her teens and pre-teens were on the right track, another baby came home.

As there wasn't much thought about birth control in those times, it's not all together unheard of for a woman to have had a "Change of Life" baby. In fact, more than a few friends I have encountered in adulthood surprised their nearly middle-aged parents. We "Babies" are all a lot alike. A little spoiled, (or a lot if you are me), a little indulged, and either protected to the point of suffocation or just let loose upon the world in utter parental exhaustion.

But growing up, I don't remember any kids like me. Everyone else's mothers were young and tall and thin and wore a lot of hair spray over their jet black or bleach blonde bouffant hairdos. They wore patent-leather boots and wore fur-trimmed jackets, just like my Barbie doll. They drove their children around to all kinds of activities and fun things to do that I was not privy to. Did I mention that they were young? They were. Looking back, this most likely is an exaggerated image, but that's the way it seemed to me, an exaggerated group of go-go dancer moms that looked more like Goldie Hawn dancing with paint all over her body than Ruth Buzzi sitting on a park bench with a hair net.

Of course my mother certainly did not look like Ruth Buzzi. Looking at pictures of her from those times, I see a woman with chestnut brown hair that was loose and not very starchy. She dressed casually in slacks and wore almost no make-up, but she had a healthy glow. She was not rail thin like Twiggy, but she was normal looking. Very normal looking as I see her now. And quite pretty.

But back then I was embarrassed. That my mother didn't drive, that she didn't go to the PTO meetings or pal around with the other moms. She didn't have time to go for out for lunch or coffee, she didn't smoke, and my dad did all the grocery shopping since he worked at the A&P. She shopped for clothes by phone, looking at the ads in the *Sunday Journal* and then calling Shepard's or Cherry & Webb; she used my father's credit card or paid cash on delivery. (Remember COD?)

She looked more mature, sure, but she didn't look old. Probably because we are now about the same age, and I certainly don't look old. I don't know why it bothered me so, that my mother was older. Probably because other kids noticed it too. "Is that your Mother or your Grandmother?" someone asked me once in first grade when my mother was waiting for me at the bus stop. I couldn't breathe, like someone gave me a sucker punch. I didn't answer. I didn't want them to know.

So certainly my mother was not like the others, cool, smoking cigarettes and chewing gum and barely 30 years old. Thinking of it now, it sounds like those other moms were a bunch of child bride ignoramuses, but I'm sure that's just the bitterness talking.

If my mother knew about my embarrassment, she never let on. She was always there for me when I needed her, and though I no longer clung next to her for protection and comfort when we were out, I knew she would be there if ever I changed my mind. As I grew up I considered her as one would her cook, servant, or lady in waiting. I'm embarrassed by the cruelty and how I took her for granted. Now I am just so thankful every day that she's still with us, that she can live an independent, or mostly independent life with my father, that all of her grandchildren and great grand-children adore her, that my daughter is so closely bonded with her and so proud of her that it makes me feel like even more a heel for the way I treated her through the years.

I became a mother for the first time at 36, not so far from 40 but in a world where most people have children later in life, after college, working for a while, saving up. It took us a long time to get Julia, two years of trying and one pregnancy of bed rest combined with all kinds of other associated anxieties from losing a pregnancy the year before. I always thought I would be the coolest mom. I would never treat my child like a little kid, would always communicate to her on an appropriate level without baby-talk and "Do it because I said so," attitudes taking over. And I would participate in her life, not be a mere spectator and well-wisher. I've done it all: PTO, PTA, everything from planning student events, to weeding the school gardens, to helping the teachers, to fundraising and making sure I'm there for nearly every soccer, softball, and basketball game. I always try to make sure that Julia, as an only child, is involved with her friends and the community. My husband was the first one to change her diaper as I was doped up on Percocet after an unusually long C-section. My husband Jeremy is the epitome of modern fatherhood. My father still doesn't hold babies until they can hold their own heads up for fear of hurting them with what we all like to refer to as his shovel hands, great spanking tools I might add. Jeremy always took Julia for a few hours on the weekend on some adventure, partly to give me a break but mostly because he really wanted to. Their bond is strong and I hope it continues to be as she matures. She adores her father, as I did mine. And she fears him enough, for he is the disciplinarian in the family, like my father was. The extent of my adventures with my dad included him taking me for ice cream around the corner at Josette's, but only if I nagged him into it. Of course I was often prodded by one or more older siblings who also wanted a treat. I remember sitting in the front seat of our Chevy Impala, and not having to even wear a seatbelt then. My father's arm and his shovel hand were my seatbelt, holding me back if we happened to stop short to take a sharp turn. I felt as protected as if I had side airbags and a booster seat at my service. And it didn't even cross my mind that my father was older too. He was forty three when I was born, but somehow that didn't matter. I had an old mom and vowed never to be an old mom myself.

You can imagine my surprise and disbelief then, when my darling fifth grader told me on the night before we headed to a field trip to the Pequot Museum in Connecticut with the entire fifth grade at Anna McCabe Elementary School, "Mom, is it okay if I'm not in your group tomorrow?"

"Why Jules, that's the reason I'm coming, so you can be in my group." I could feel it coming—the sucker punch to the gut.

"Well ... I'm not trying to hurt your feelings, but you're not really one of the cool Moms."

Once I caught my breath I repeated the phrase. "One of the cool moms. The cool moms. Not one of the cool moms." There was no comeback for this. I had been slapped, and the sting of it almost knocked me over. I immediately thought of my mother waiting for me at the bus stop with her cable knit cardigan with tortoise shell fasteners, looking all baggy and old after a day of slave labor.

"And who are these so-called cool moms?" I finally blurted, keeping my composure as best as I could.

"Forget it, Mom. Forget it."

Oh no you don't, Missy. I am not going to forget this. This is war.

"No, Julia, tell me. Tell me who the cool moms are and how they are just so cool. The moms who let you do whatever you want, are those the cool moms? Because if that's the case I will never be a cool mom. And just who said I'm not a cool mom? Do your friends say that?" This was the Inquisition, and I was going to get to the bottom of this treason. All of the sweet pre-pubescent faces of her friends, classmates, everyone at Anna McCabe Elementary School flipped through my mind as I tried to identify suspects.

"No one, Mom! Forget it."

"Oh I'm not going to forget it. I want to know!" I could hear my husband rustling dishes in the background, probably preparing himself for an intervention. But I didn't care. This was horrendous, this notion of me not being cool. Of course I'm cool. I take these brats wherever they want to go whenever they want to. I cheer them on and I buy their baked goods at all their bake sales, I treat them like my own flesh and blood. Not cool?

My daughter just put her head down, regretting the mere utterance, which is as it should be.

I made a desperate attempt at retaliation, one that may backfire if not done right. "Maybe I will just stay home tomorrow then, or go to work, if I'm not cool."

"No Mom! I'm sorry!" I was getting to her. Excellent. "It's just that you don't always let us do stuff…"

"Because I'm responsible for you. I'm the chaperone. Do you know what that means?" This I state with pomposity beyond imagination. But I'm wounded. Terribly, terribly wounded.

Of course we had a great time on the field trip, despite my ridiculous tantrum the night before. The kids in my group were both adorable and major pains in the butt, as all fifth graders must be. Some of them actually wanted to spend time with my uncoolness, including one Julia, I might add.

I still bring up the cool mom tag, much to both my daughter and my husband's dismay, but as a joke. Really. As a matter of fact, the day after the field trip Julia shared a little something with me on the car ride home. One of her friends told her that she was lucky to have a Mom and Dad that were both funny. Not cool? Oh well, I'll take what I can get.

"Well Julia, do you feel lucky? Do you?" my best Clint Eastwood. Of course she does. She just doesn't know it yet.

My Parents at Tony's 100th birthday celebration in 1993.

PICKLED PEPPERS

F ood is such an important element in all cultures, for the obvious reasons of sustenance, of course. But there's more.

Preparing food, the rituals of cooking, presenting, consuming, hold such archetypal images of nurturing, caring, and providing. Mothers and daughters for thousands of years have prepared food together. Italian-American families hold many great traditions, to be carried down with hopes of preserving our culture, what makes us special. My mother learned from her mother and older sisters, as did I. Sadly, I have yet to pass on many of these traditions to my almost 12-year-old daughter; although I know the time will come when preparing for holidays and other special occasions will pique her interest enough to want to learn. When she's not listening to her music or dribbling a basketball, that is.

What I love about preparing food most, other than eating, is that this preparation is something we must do; whether we are angry, bitter, depressed, right or wrong, we must eat and food must be prepared. We can argue later, but for now let's just get these peppers sliced. And who knows, maybe we will find common ground as we cut and dice and stir.

My mother called me early one Saturday morning, before I could get any caffeine into my nervous system and thus make any reasonably sound judgments.

"We're going to do the pickled peppers for the café. You still wanna learn how to make them?"

"Um, yeah, sure. When?" I always wanted to learn how my mother made the tangy green peppers that garnished the antipasto my father prepared each Easter, Christmas, Thanksgiving and any other holiday we could fit it into. My husband loves them, piling them into salads, munching sandwiches of them along with chunks of extra sharp, extra hard provolone cheese, paper-thin slivers of prosciutto ham and thick crusty slices of Italian bread. The kind of bread with crust so sharp that it cuts the roof of your mouth when you bite it, allowing a combination of vinegary peppers and salty ham and cheese to penetrate your palate until it itches and throbs in culinary ecstasy.

Learning how to make pickled peppers would be a chance to spend time with my Mom alone. Except there was a "we" involved. Too late, I had already said yes. Damn coffee.

"Tomorrow morning, early. Pick me up and we'll meet Donna at the café around eight."

Donna. The Café. That Crow.

Today at 88, we now all call my mother the Old Crow. She's earned the right to be ornery at times, to turn off the filtering system from her brain to her tongue. To spit gum out on the sidewalk without any of us scolding her about her gum removal etiquette.

Donna is my sister. At the time, we had hardly spoken a word in over a year. The reasons make no sense, except that all my siblings suffer from a condition in which we hold each other to incredibly high, largely unachievable standards impossible to reach, never mind maintain. Disappointment in each other's actions, along with snap judgments and second guessing motives go along with this malady. Feeling victimized by those with unrealistic standards towards us tops off this charming tendency we all possess. In other words, ego and pride can sometimes take over well beyond healthy measure.

The café is Donna's café, the Mezzanine Café. Situated in the middle of a medical building, my sister, with some help from the Crow, prepares sandwiches, coffee, desserts and Testa family Italian specialties for the doctors, medical techs, patients and other assorted tenants and visitors. My parents helped my sister buy this café, since she is without a husband and was previously raising her daughters on a school bus driver's salary and child support for the last 10 years. Of course my parents didn't mention to this to any of us prior to doing this, as another great Testa personality trait is secrecy. This one threw all of the dysfunctional siblings, me included, into an uproar. Of course if we all did try to discuss this together as a family, each of us would feel the urge to take control and offer his or her own ideas, to the point where Donna and my parents would have regretted bringing up the subject. Again, many thanks to the creators of my gene pool. I'm not sure if this is all due to nature, nurture, or a delicately blended combination of both.

Each October, Donna gets ready for the holidays by jarring a colossal batch of pickled peppers and selling them to her patrons for Thanksgiving and Christmas. The recipe is easy but the process to prepare them must be executed meticulously, or you will end up with mushy, discolored pickled peppers. No one wants to bite into a limp pepper. Properly pickled peppers must be crisp and tangy and have a warm olive-green hue, transforming from their bright cool emerald color as they pickle. The bell jars that they are packed into naturally display imperfections as well as quality. You can't hide a sub-par pepper in a glass bell jar.

I had agreed to help Crow and Donna and I would live up to my word. No hedging or backing out, or what would everyone think? What would they say? Slacker Pat says she will help you one day and doesn't follow through the next. Plus, I really wanted to know how to make the peppers.

As the youngest of five, I didn't always get the same opportunities to prepare food my older sisters did. I could execute rudimentary tasks, like rolling out dough for cinnamon pinwheels, sifting dry ingredients like flour and baking powder, or dropping blobs of ricotta cheese over steamy lasagna noodles (with supervision).

But pouring gallon jugs of white vinegar into cauldrons of boiling water, adding precise measures of salt and sugar—and not confusing the two—required strength, focus and the ability to flip hot glass jars upside down without dropping them. Back in those days, when we didn't have a dishwasher to sterilize the jars at the start, my mother boiled the jars, dropping them gently in and out of boiling water with large heavy metal tongs. Not tasks for her baby to try. But I did get to watch.

We drove to the café in silence as I slurped down an iced coffee. I tried to think of things to talk about once we arrived to avoid potentially uncomfortable silences. My mother gazed out the window and tried not to criticize my driving.

I had never been inside the café as I was initially opposed to my parents making such a substantial loan on a fixed income. It looked like a real place where food was prepared and served on a daily basis. Nothing magical or mysterious. Very charming, actually. My niece ran over and hugged me and I felt like a big schmuck for not seeing her last Christmas, or on her last birthday.

Donna always worked hard at whatever she did, and with the stamina of a draught horse—a Clydesdale dragging a ton of bricks without complaint or even breaking a sweat. She deserves a chance to be successful. After years of being a faithful wife, then a heartbroken ex-wife with two girls to raise, then three girls to raise when she took in a foster child and ended up adopting her.

Who was I, someone who may appear to possess things my sister longed for, things she had at one time, but may be out of reach at the moment? Who was I to resent her opportunity to be content? It's not what I intended when I began my usual judging and criticizing, but it probably appears that way to everyone else.

Donna was sitting at a serving table, slicing peppers into thick strips, throwing the stems and the seeds, along with any yellow or red streaked slices into one giant aluminum bowl, and the strips to be pickled into another giant aluminum bowl. She looked up but didn't say anything.

My mother got right to work, scrubbing up like a surgeon, then inspecting the boiling water and vinegar combination that will serve as the pickling agent, making sure the salt bowl was labeled salt and the sugar bowl was labeled sugar. Each jar will get stuffed with the green pepper strips, and then get filled to the brim with hot water and vinegar. Each jar will then receive one spoonful of sugar and one spoonful of salt. This is the tricky part. You don't want two spoons of salt and no sugar or two spoons of sugar and no salt in your pepper jar.

"What should I do?" I was hesitant to join into this well-oiled process, for fear of ruining two bushels of green peppers that would equate to hours of labor and hundreds of dollars in gross income.

"You can take over here while I get the jars ready," my sister said softly, looking at me as if she wasn't sure if she could trust me after the bad feelings that had passed between us.

The smell of hot vinegar felt unpleasant at first, but cleansing once your nostrils got acclimated to the tingle. I sat down, acquainted myself with the paring knife, and got into a slicing groove.

Small talk in the manner of preparation steps and requirements turned into general small talk, then to the final moment, the knowing look between two sisters when their mother said something comical; something they laughed together about 40 years ago and was still funny. Yes, we were being a bit critical, but all in good fun, and unbeknownst to my mother. I think.

Actually I think that Old Crow executed a well-planned covert operation to bring two of her girls together—it worked seamlessly.

THE HUNGER GAMES—
BAD CHICKEN

L
ast week I was in danger of contaminating 12 pounds of butterfly split
boneless chicken breasts. How you may ask? I did not move it from my
mother's refrigerator to my freezer for at least 52 hours.

My parents sweetly and considerately supply me with packages of
beautiful and easy-to-cook breasts from a local Italian market. These
breasts are now a staple at my house, and since I know nothing about
meat—who sells good meat, what good cuts are—I am eternally grateful
for this favor, even if it does mean that my 91 year old father ventures out
in the car for the five mile round trip drive to the market. He enjoys it, as
he has so few opportunities to take care of others these days. He calls in
advance and places the order for me, making the whole process effortless
on my part.

I have offered to go with him, or go instead of him to pick up the
chicken, because I do feel angst each time he puts the pedal to the metal,
so to speak. But I don't mind going to my parents to pick up the package,
carefully wrapped by the butcher in multiple layers of cellophane packaging,
separated individually by Styrofoam trays. No Going Green here, except that
it's all wrapped in a paper bag. It's old fashioned butcher packaging, circa
1950. Very airtight, and all throw-away.

The issue I encounter with this arrangement is that I have to pick this
package up as soon as possible after its arrival, even beforehand if possible.
Because heaven forbid the chicken spoils as it lies tightly wrapped in the
fridge for those countless minutes or even hours before I get there. The
cellophane must be unraveled, the chicken rescued and rinsed, then dried
and repackaged in zip lock bags in appropriate portions, labeled and frozen
as quickly as possible. This ritual must take place no later than 12 hours after
pickup. But there are obstacles. There are always obstacles.

Chicken pickup day may be big doings at their house, and it's important to me of course. But it's one in about seven trillion other things I need to tend to.

My mother calls the day before pickup, Friday evening at precisely 7 p.m., or 19:00 for those of you on military time.

"Yeah, your father's going to get the chicken tomorrow morning. You can pick it up anytime Saturday. When you get a chance." Sounds harmless enough doesn't it?

"Okay Ma. I'll be by tomorrow. We're painting Julia's room, so I may get there later in the day, or Sunday."

"Oh, it doesn't matter. When you get here you get here." Her tone may be nonchalant, but I know better.

"I'll call you tomorrow, Ma, and let you know."

The games begin.

Saturday is spent trying to figure out how to paint walls and molding without calling someone I can pay to do it for me. I can do this. We can do this.

2 p.m. (14:00), the phone rings.

"Hello Mother." I brace myself.

"Yeah, I was just wondering if you were going to come and get the chicken today or not."

"Well, we're kind of in the middle of this room painting. I'll be there tomorrow morning to get it."

"Okay, when you get here, you get here. I just thought I'd call because you don't want that chicken to go bad in the refrigerator. It's a lot of chicken."

"It'll be okay for a day, Ma. I'll call you in the morning. We should be in a better place with this room by then."

"Well all right then." Translation: you are taking your life into your own hands by delaying this chicken pick-up.

"Don't worry Ma."

"Oh I'm not worrying about anything." Her effortless lies chill me to the bone.

Sunday does not prove better than Saturday as far as priming and painting go. Progress is slow, and my daughter is getting a little too used to sleeping on a blow-up mattress downstairs, spending most of her time on her iPod FaceTiming her friends versus getting any rest. Her territory and its accompanying clutter spread like through our family room like wildfire.

High Noon: The phone rings. I catch my breath as I almost trip on a drop cloth.

"I know, Ma. The chicken."

"Yeah, well you know, this chicken isn't going to stay good forever. It needs to be unpacked. Or it's going to go bad."

24 hours have passed since the chicken arrived at their house. It has been refrigerated for all but for the 20 minutes it took my father to drive two and a half miles home from the market at 25 miles per hour.

"I will be there tomorrow to get the chicken, Ma. Just keep it chilled. Please."

I hear my father in the background, "When is she going to get that chicken? Soon it'll go bad . . ." his voice tapers off. I'm sure he has his head stuck in the fridge looking at the package in question.

When I get a call from a good friend inviting me to the beach on Monday, I accept with no thought whatsoever about the bacteria-laden poultry at my mother's. Later I break into a cold sweat when I realize that if I go two plus days without getting that chicken out, I may be in for more danger than I can imagine. I fear the confrontation with my parents. I must tell them the truth. No use sugar-coating it. Or coating it in breadcrumbs for that matter.

I dial the number, praying desperately for them to be out so I can leave a message.

"Are you comin' to get this chicken?" My mother demands as soon as she realizes who is on the other end of the phone.

"Well, about that", I stammer, "I'm going to get it tomorrow, but not until late afternoon. I'm going to the beach." There I've said it. Silence.

"Well you know, this chicken isn't going to keep forever."

"I will stop there on my way home from the beach. I promise."

"You don't need to promise me anything. I just figured that if it stays out too long you know, it'll go bad. Do what you want, though." Her emotional investment in my well-being has reached an end. I'm on my own now.

Maybe I shouldn't go to the beach. But Julia wants to go, and I want to spend some time with my friend and her family. My husband has gallantly offered to do the painting while we're gone so the project will keep its momentum. Other than Labor Day, it's the last Monday holiday this summer.

Yes, it's a holiday in Rhode Island on this Monday—VJ Day, once called Victory over Japan Day, but now called Victory Day to remove some of magnitude of the occasion. Makes it feel light and sunny. Because victory is a good thing, isn't it?

We are the only state in the union which still celebrates bringing nuclear collapse to Japan during World War II. Not for sentimental reasons, of course.

We just celebrate it because it gives us another Monday off in the summer. I kid you not. Only in Rhode Island. Massachusetts celebrates Patriots' Day each April, but that has nothing to do with nuclear obliteration. At least I don't think it does.

That night my dreams are haunted by giant raw headless birds, shaking their wings at me, clicking and clucking their absent tongues in disgust. When are you going to pick up that chicken? I wake in a cold sweat, with sheets wrapped around my ankles in shackles.

After a lovely, guilt-ridden day at the beach, my daughter and I head over to Mimi and Papa's to pick up the dreaded chicken that has been lying out in the hot sun since Saturday. Or tightly wrapped and refrigerated. One or the other, I forget.

5 p.m. (17:00): we are almost there. I stop at the ATM to get the money for said chicken so that I can pay my parents. I'm in the drive up line when my phone rings. I see the name, and apparently my subconscious takes over because I hang up by accident. Stop the madness, my soul pleads.

I could just drive there and not call back. It would be faster and I'm only three minutes away. But I can't do it. My honesty is a blessing … and a curse.

"I'm coming!" I half yell, and half laugh in exasperation. "I'm coming for the ridiculous chicken now! Do you think it will hold for another 30 seconds till I pull into your driveway and make it up the steps? Hurry and open the door so I can just dash in and get it!"

"Oh be quiet, you and your chicken," my mother says. "If I knew it would take you this long I would have repacked it and kept it in the freezer for you." Again with the lies.

"But then what would you have to call me about?" I ask innocently.

Thanks for the chicken you two. It's delicious. And if you don't hear from me tomorrow, I've probably died from Salmonella poisoning.

Alphonse sending a message over and out
to his girl back in Providence

KING OF THE ROAD

Yes, this is my mother's story, not my father's. But my mother would not be the person she is today without having this man travel along by her side. She has been the passenger while he has been the driver all these years, but that's beginning to change now. I'm not sure how much longer my father will be in the driver's seat. But the Crow is willing and ready to take over the wheel. Her journey would not be the same without him.

My father turned 91 yesterday. Longevity runs through his family tree. His father Tony was 103 when he died in 1996. His mother Jenny was 94 when she passed six years earlier, and his sister, my Auntie Dot, just hit 92 this past June.

Big Al, as opposed to Young Al, my 62 year-old brother, is one lucky guy. Blessed, you might say. He still drives, though thankfully, not very far around town in Johnston and the surrounding area. My niece just informed me that he recently took his driver's license renewal test and passed. Thank you Rhode Island Department of Motor Vehicles.

I assume this was not a road test, but there's a part of me who would like to meet the DMV person who gave him a passing grade. So what if he still remembers the rules of the road? His reflexes are not what they used to be, his fingers become numb as he tries to clutch the steering wheel and a few months back, when he had one arm in a sling due to a fractured wrist, he did not stay off the road. With my mother riding shotgun, they get around somehow, refusing our persistent attempts to chauffeur them.

So yes, I'd like to ask the DMV person what on earth they were thinking when they renewed my father's license. Another part of me is grateful, as the alternative is worse to consider. What if he failed? What then? What would he and his 88-year-old wife do? Getting to his umpteen doctors' appointments each week would be impossible. You see, my father can pretty much claim sole responsibility for the continuing prosperity of the U.S. pharmaceutical industry these past 20 years. It needs him. And groceries. Who would run out twice a day to purchase those essential bags full of escarole on special that my mother is pressured to cook before the end of each week? And what about the broccoli rabe? The shredded wheat, and those cases of canned plum tomatoes for gravy? How many sales would be missed? Again the Rhode Island economy depends on my father and his trips in support of supermarkets and farm stands, big and small.

Certainly among their five children, the two of them would have little trouble completing their errands. But it means my father would be forced to depend on us, after we have depended on him for years and years and years—and still do sometimes. But it's much less often now.

My mother, who never drove, never wrote a check, or paid a bill, is less resistant to being cared for, at least in some ways. Not my dad though.

There isn't a huge demand for their babysitting services anymore. Or their advice—solicited or not. They don't clean up after us, feed us or check up on us. We check up on them. Little by little, they have cared for us less and we have taken on more, usually amid much confusion or after their errors in judgment or memory force us to act. Between us all we can do it.

The price for taking this responsibility is steep. And while I'm able and ready to help, I'm not so sure I'm willing.

Not because I'm an arrogant selfish child. Strike that. I possess some definite level of selfishness here. Once we kids swoop in and take over, the end of everything I've ever known and believed as permanent will dissipate. With nothing and no one to take care of, without the freedom to drive to the corner store for milk and ice cream at will, my father will cease to exist. He will become an old man who can't take care of himself anymore. He'll be more of an item on my To Do list than a force to be reckoned with. I don't know if I can cope with losing him.

Of course, I've had my dad longer than most. Most of my close friends no longer have their fathers—or their mothers—anymore. I'm the lucky one. There has been no sudden death to mourn, no nursing home or hospital to deal with, no disease to ravage away their flesh and my sanity. Just a little old man and a little old lady to take care of.

Big Al is a lucky guy. He still has his wife and his home and his driver's license. He pays his own bills and tends to his own affairs. His grandchildren love him, his great-grandchildren know him enough to remember him, and he has lived to see his great, great-granddaughter. And he's probably got another few years of driving left in him. I have to keep reminding myself how fast the time will fly. When my daughter was born, everyone told us to enjoy every moment; she will be grown up before we know it. No one warned me about enjoying every moment with my parents. But I figured it out;luckily it's not too late.

The Wedding Reception on Dover Street. Maid of Honor, my Auntie Dot, is on the far left, Best Man Uncle Danny on the far right. My Grandma Jenny prepared all of the food and decor that day for some 200 guests.

THE PIZZELLA LESSON, OR
WHERE WE END, FOR NOW

My mother is an amazing person. If you've read any of this, I challenge you to disagree. She was loved and indulged as a child, lost her mother tragically, met and married the man she'd love for the next 70 years (and more); she has children, grand-children, great grand-children, and as of now, a great great-grand-daughter. She's worked incredibly hard, suffered tragically, and discovered herself in the process. She now takes care of the man who took care of her, or calls the shots now, as she likes to put it. She is the gentlest caregiver to children that I've ever known, and makes a profound impact on each life she has brought into this world in ways that cannot be properly expressed in words. She is still my teacher, even though I can be a pompous know-it-all with little patience and much sarcasm. She loved me so much that she allowed me to find myself, and keep myself. But she still loves me anyway.

She is my daughter's playmate, and has not only taught her to sketch, but to laugh and be silly and to be herself, no matter how outrageous. Julia is a better person for having Mimi in her life, as someone who adores her, but makes sure she doesn't take herself too seriously.

Spending a Saturday afternoon with my mother making pizzelle, pretty much sums up our relationship today. Not that we spend each Saturday baking. But it's the dynamic of mother and daughter that will never leave us. I don't want it to. I want to get all the Italian baking and cooking lessons that I can, so I can hear about my family, how they managed, what they thought.

I have always been fascinated with the pizzelle iron as a child. My mother got her iron forty three years ago on her 25th wedding anniversary as a gift from her mother-in-law, my Grandma Jenny. I told my mother that when she croaks I get the iron. I talk in this 'tough egg' manner when I don't want to confront the thought of ever losing her. It beats the alternative of feeling weepy at the thought of my mother not being there when I call her, of no one to tell me when I'm acting ridiculous, or hugging me gently on the way out the door and calling me a scallywag, whatever that is.

As a child, I spent countless afternoons watching my mother at the pizzelle iron, as she pressed the batter down and wiped the edges of the iron with a cloth to avoid ridges at the ends of the waffle cookies. I was never allowed to touch the iron, which is probably what drove me to want to make them now. At 48 I'm probably old enough now. But you would never know it.

"Be careful of that iron and don't touch it.

"Don't let it stay down too long or they'll burn.

"You want to make sure they cook enough. Wait until they're tan."

"Don't touch that iron with your hands, you'll get burnt."

"Careful, I'll do it for you."

My 88 year old mother anxiously watched as I used the iron like a big girl. A big, middle-aged, old lady girl. The dynamic has not changed and it never will. I'm glad for it as it is a constant I can depend on for a while longer, as long as I am fortunate enough to be a phone call or a drive down the road away.

Christmas 2012. The Old Crow looks great for 88. Here with
my great, great niece Rylee on her lap, and my daughter
Julia in the background (photo by Dawne O'Brien)

EPILOGUE

Pizzelle are part of special family celebrations like weddings, Easter, baby showers, and Christmas, any occasion that brings family together. I love pizzelle because they aren't too sweet, you can make them any flavor you like within reason (we did chocolate and pumpkin spice for thanksgiving), they are great with a cup of coffee or tea, and, now that I am a big girl, they are really easy to make.

<u>The Old Crow's Recipe</u>

6 eggs
2 sticks of butter or margarine (she uses margarine)
1 cup sugar
3 cups flour
4 teaspoons of baking powder
Flavoring of your choice—1 teaspoon of either vanilla, orange, lemon, anise, rum or almond extract.
For chocolate, use ¼ cup baking cocoa. Or, you can toss in a shot of anisette, or rum, or whiskey.
Use 1 tsp. cinnamon, 1 tsp. nutmeg and ¼ tsp. clove for pumpkin pie flavor, or use pumpkin pie spice.

- Melt the margarine, then let it cool, but not solidify. Once cooled, beat in eggs.
- Then beat in the dry ingredients and sugar, along with the flavoring. For chocolate, take some baking cocoa (1/4 cup) and some water and mix in a small bowl until the cocoa is dissolved, then add to the pizzelle batter.
- The batter should be stiff, but not doughy. It should be able to stand up when you spoon it up. A little thicker than a meringue. This from

someone who doesn't bake, but loves to eat. It's airy like meringue but has a little more body.

- Preheat the pizzelle iron. Usually a little light on top will light when it's ready. You can spray it with PAM very lightly before you start, but if the batter's right they really won't stick.
- Put a heaping tablespoon full of batter on the center of the hot iron and press. Give about 30 seconds and lift. The cookie should be tannish, not too white. Of course with the chocolate you have to be a little more careful not to overcook. You should be able to lift the cookie up with a fork and place it on a plate. It should pick up without drooping or being too doughy.
- Pizzelle have to cool for a few hours at least. Spread them out on the platter after cooking versus keeping them in a big stack.
- Once they are cool, you can sprinkle them with powdered sugar. The longer they stay out the crisper they will be. Don't wrap them up too quickly or they will be soft, which you don't want. Pizzelle should be thin and crisp, not soggy.

Pizzelle can be stored in a tin for at least a week, maybe more. They look pretty on a plate wrapped in cellophane with a ribbon. That's usually how they are displayed in bakeries or on the table at an Italian wedding or baby shower. Although, as the Old Crow says, it's how they taste, not what they look like.

CPSIA information can be obtained at www.ICGtesting.com
Printed in the USA
BVOW030259310513

322056BV00002B/7/P